EXPLORING CAREERS IN VIDEO AND DIGITAL VIDEO

By
PAUL ALLMAN

The Rosen Publishing Group, Inc.
NEW YORK

Published in 1985, 1987, 1989, 1998 by The Rosen Publishing Group, Inc.
29 East 21st Street, New York, NY 10010

Copyright 1985, 1987, 1989, 1998 by Paul Allman

All rights reserved. No part of this book may be reproduced in any form without permission in writing from the publisher, except by a reviewer.

Photo credits: pp. 5, 53, 65, 70 by Monica Howard Photo. P. 58 by AP/Wide World. P. 79 by Paul Allman Photo, courtesy of Teatown Editing, New York. All others by author.

Revised Edition 1998

Library of Congress Cataloging-in-Publication Data

Allman, Paul.
    Exploring careers in video and digital video.
    Includes index.
    Summary: Describes the various careers available in television and how to acquire the necessary training and preparation.
    1. Television—Vocational guidance. [1. Television—Vocational guidance. 2. Vocational guidance] I. Title.
PN1992.55.A45   1984 791.43'023'0973 84-9801
ISBN 0-8239-2542-0

Manufactured in the United States of America

To
James J. Allman

About the Author

Paul Allman received a B.A. in Film and Television from the University of Iowa. Since that time he has worked nonstop in radio, film, television, and theater in the United States and abroad. He now lives in New York City.

Contents

Introduction	1
1. "Roll Tape!": The Birth of the Video Industry	3
2. Jobs: Where and Why	8
3. The Training Ground	12
4. Name Your Poison	26
5. Having What It Takes	87
6. The Rewards	96
7. Being Your Own Boss	100
8. Rock and Reel	113
9. The Tough Get Started	121
10. The Digital Video Revolution	130
Appendix	133
Index	140

Introduction

This book was first published during a tremendous boom in video production, when anything could have happened to the new cable industry, and when video cassette recorders (VCRs) were just beginning to show up next to the television set. It was always my belief that whatever happened to the technology of video production, a hired team of humans would always be needed to manage each production. Not only has the number of jobs in television remained constant during this period of remarkable technological advancement in the video industry, but those advancements have *increased* the number of jobs available to those planning a career in video.

The video business will continue to increase its flexibility through the next century. The VCR has had a lot to do with the transition because it allows us to watch a program whenever we want to. The remote control device allows us to scan a wide variety of choices in no time at all, and as a result we have become a society of sophisticated viewers who "graze" the television channels and slip easily from one situation into another.

In some parts of the United States, hundreds of channels are available to choose from, including satellite broadcasts from faraway places. Don't like what's offered on the tube? Rent a tape from your local video store, or plug in one of your many home movies.

Introduction

Additionally, the digital video revolution is changing the way we shoot, edit, and distribute programming content. It also represents more ways for you to get into the business. Your computer skills, honed at home, can now be an asset as producers who are taking advantage of various multimedia formats search far and wide for competent computer programmers, software designers, special effects wizards, and videographic designers.

But the golden rule that has been true for the last ninety years, and will be true well past the year 2000, is that no matter how the media are delivered to the public's home, office, or to public spaces, somebody has to think it up, write it down, light it, shoot it, and edit it. In this book, I will describe all of the jobs and responsibilities in each of these phases of video production. It's your job to figure out what *you* want to do in this wide-open, fast-breaking world of video and digital video.

1

"Roll Tape!": The Birth of the Video Industry

Whatever happened to "Roll 'em!"? In the old days, directors hollered those magic words through a megaphone. Now, that stereotype of the film director is obsolete. The new breed of directors has adopted the less majestic call of "Roll tape." And instead of bellowing at the actors who are baking under the lights, the director probably has her back to the actors and her eyes glued to a video playback monitor.

The video industry has captured a lot of territory that used to belong to film. In soundstages and editing rooms everywhere, the clatter of gears and sprockets has been replaced by the growl of a video tape recorder and the steady whir of the fans that cool the electronics. The crack of the clapstick, which demanded silence until the cry of "Action!", has all but disappeared. *Why?* That is the question asked by many professionals who miss the smell of unexposed film. The fact is that video is unbelievably popular, and there are specific reasons for that.

The changeover from film to video has been noticeable in the nonbroadcast production facilities of corporations and smaller businesses. Not only have they adopted the new video format for their training tapes and promotional material, but because of the many advantages of video, more and more businesses are also hiring in-house producers.

The primary advantage of video production is the relatively low cost. There was a time when film stock could be bought, shot, and processed at a competitive rate, and it is no surprise that during that time the video industry was not particularly strong. But in the 1970s, for many reasons, the cost of film nearly doubled.

As a result, big business was ready to stop making training films because they were too expensive and therefore cost-inefficient. But they ultimately discovered that, for the cost of completing one thirty-minute 16 mm film, they could outfit themselves with a $3/4$-inch video tape recorder and a decent portable color camera. Many companies did just that, and saved a fortune on production costs. A sixty-minute cassette cost about twenty dollars and could be reused.

Another advantage was even more satisfying than the low cost of equipment and tape stock: video produces immediate results. As soon as you complete a take, you can rewind the tape and see exactly what's on it. There is no waiting for laboratories to process and print film, none of the anxiety that comes from waiting for results and wondering whether you have to reshoot. If you don't like what you see on the TV screen, you can shoot it again. This on-the-spot monitoring of the production saves a lot of time and money. And if there is any kind of equipment malfunction, it is immediately apparent and can be fixed quickly.

The dependability of video equipment is an important issue when considering that a lot of people unfamiliar with the new technology are becoming producers. One of the true marvels of basic video pro-

"Roll Tape!": The Birth of the Video Industry

Watching tape playback through the viewfinder.

duction is that the equipment is capable of doing a lot of the work for you. Most cameras are equipped with an automatic exposure setting that can guarantee an acceptable picture. Those same cameras are designed to function with a lot less light than is needed to shoot film. And the tape recorder can be set to record sound at a standard level by using what is called a limiter.

Because of these helpful functions, all that a low-budget producer has to do is turn on the power, insert a tape, turn on a light, and point the camera at whatever he wants to see. These automatic features can produce something that is basically average in quality. But the fact that they are standard features in video equipment has opened the field to many people who otherwise would never get the chance to work in media.

As you might expect, video's accessibility produced volumes of material. But at the same time the video production industry was growing, a whole new market opened up: cable television. Although it boasted fifteen or more channels, many of these channels were empty for long stretches of time. The channels that did have material were broadcasting mostly local shows produced by people who left their equipment on automatic and anchored their cameras in one place. The result was that much of cable programming looked flat, washed-out, and dull.

But because cable is broadcast via wire and not antenna, the picture was cleaner and interference-free—and it soon became clear that those "dead" channels were about to spring to life. Companies such as Time, Inc. and Ted Turner Enterprises were negotiating for them: dealing to buy every minute of a channel on cable TV. When the deals were closed and the first pictures rolled into place, television never looked the same again.

Much of the programming during the first days of television resembled the old days of radio, with quiz shows, variety shows, and some sitcoms. Now, thirty years later, cable television is doing exactly what radio did many years ago: specializing. It is now possible to tune in to channels that show only movies, or all news, one devoted solely to health programs, one for financial news, and yet another that supplies nothing but home improvement tips. Each one of these cable channels is busy filling its broadcast time with appropriate material, while even more channels are opened up to new programs.

As business adopts video technology as a tool, and as the cable industry continues to look for more broadcast material, one can guess as to the number of jobs that are opening up in the field. For every addition of a technique or a policy to a growing business, a new training tape has to be made. Every program broadcast over the air or over cable is finished as soon as the credits roll, and a new show has to fill that slot the next day. And for every business or network or cable station that produces its own material, there are more that hire production companies to satisfy the insatiable appetite for all kinds of programs.

2

Jobs: Where and Why

Although film producers and video producers deliver products that look essentially alike, the means of achieving the visible ends are vastly different. It would be oversimplifying to declare that film is the old way and video is the new way. There are a lot of similarities, and just as many technical gaps. The point of this book is not to decide whether film or video is better; the point is to bring you up to date on the business and try to give you a few leads to landing that all-important first job. So let's take a look at the quality and quantity of jobs available.

If you are not certain where you want to go and what you want to do in the television business, one of the first decisions to make is whether to work in film or video.

One basic reality about the film industry is that the real film jobs exist only on the east and west coasts. It has been that way since the early days of cinema, when Thomas Edison had a patent that specified if you wanted to make a movie, you had to pay him some money. Edison was in New Jersey, so the outlaw filmmakers left for California where the weather was better and the law was far away. Hollywood was born out of this gold rush, and it has been the same ever since.

JOBS: WHERE AND WHY

If you want to make movies today—the big, glitzy kind of movies—you'll have to deal with somebody from either New York or Hollywood. Likewise, if you're not eager to become a classic producer but you'd like employment on a big-budget picture, one of the coasts is where you'll wind up.

Often, a feature film will go on location in the Midwest or the South or someplace, to add local color. But it doesn't happen as often as you'd think, or as often as the local hotels and restaurants would like. Most films are made right in California. And all together, *not that many features are made*—maybe thirty a year in all. And many producers hire the same crews from movie to movie. That doesn't add up to a lot of work for those who don't have a book full of the right contacts.

When I graduated from college with my radio/TV degree, I had to make a decision about where to go. For reasons that will become clear later, I chose New York. But a friend of mine, who had similar experience, booked his passage to Hollywood. There was a Hollywood director by the name of Nick Meyer, who had struck it relatively big with a movie called *Time After Time*, which was adapted from a book he had written. *Time After Time* didn't make a lot of money, but it was well done and well received, and Nick Meyer was given a shot at directing *Star Trek, The Wrath of Khan*. At that time, a movie with the title "Star Trek" was almost guaranteed to reap an audience from all the Trekkie fanatics who no longer got fresh episodes of their favorite show on television. And you could pretty much guarantee that a good portion of this audience would see the movie more than once. *Wrath of Khan* would make money, and Nicholas Meyer would make more movies. Meyer was a graduate of our very own film school and, during a visit to the Film Department, graciously invited all interested students to give him a call if we should be in his neighborhood.

My friend at film school decided to be the first. He packed his bags for Hollywood. He called a few old friends who had moved to Hollywood a few years back to make it big, but had had to settle on making enough money for a convertible couch that people could sleep on when *they* came to Hollywood to make it big. My friend dreamed of sitting in meetings, taking notes and sharing inside jokes with the director, strolling onto the set with a clipboard in his hand and a stopwatch around his neck, his head bent and nodding in agreement with the director who had taken the graduate's brilliant advice about a crucial plot idea and gone on to win an Oscar *precisely* because of that advice and mentioned the graduate's name during the acceptance speech.

Well, he made his call and he got his job, our graduate. His job was this: While Nick Meyer was encouraging Khan to show some wrath, my friend was hired to sit in Nick Meyer's apartment to water the plants and feed the dog. He never even got close to the set.

There is one thing you should understand: My graduate friend was *lucky*! Because what Nick Meyer did was really and truly incredible. He didn't have to make that promise when he visited the Film Department. He could have said, "I worked my tail off and hustled like you'd never believe to *earn* this position," which he did. But what Nick Meyer was really saying was that, despite his hard work and his remarkable creative talent, he had to be lucky to get where he was, and he knew it. Meyer can't help a fellow alumni when it comes to talent or guts, but he could give your lucky stars a little shove. This says a lot about Nick Meyer. It also says a lot about the business. If you want to make Hollywood your home and you want to work there, be prepared to consider yourself lucky if you get to feed a good man's dog.

Because the film production workplace is split, chances of finding work in major film productions are slim. A big reason for this is that "major film production" accounts for only three kinds of products: feature films, television commercials, and network series. Those are really the last areas for 35 mm filmmaking, and it's no coincidence that all three are big moneymakers. They have to be, because 35 mm is expensive. Your movie, commercial, or series had better make a bundle of money, because it's going to *cost* a bundle to shoot. With the high cost of this kind of filmmaking, the limited amount of production that comes with it, and the geographic limitations of the workplace, the ratio of people who go looking for this kind of work to those that find it is very, very high.

This is where the realities of the video industry come in. Especially as someone new to media, you have more opportunities to get work in video than in film. Between the two coasts are a lot of places to work, all the way from Dallas to Madison, Wisconsin. Nearly every city has a local television station that serves as a network affiliate. That means local production, beginning with pre–production organization, studio or location shooting, and postproduction editing. Most of this work is put into the local news. And this sort of production happens daily, employing a lot of people in all departments, and the source of it is probably a few miles from you wherever you might be. That means you don't have to go far to find that first job that will give you the experience that can take you eventually into the larger markets.

3

The Training Ground

There is always a problem getting the initial experience that can lead to your first job: you can't get the job without the experience, and you can't get the experience without a job. But there are ways around that catch. You know that *somebody's* getting that job. It may as well be you.

In Chapter 1, I mentioned that the low cost of video equipment helped many local organizations to join the ranks of producers with a relatively small investment. The stress is on the world *local*. These places are numerous and nearby. For the most part, they are made up of colleges and universities, cable access studios, and local TV stations.

UNIVERSITIES AND COLLEGES

A college with a decent media department is a wonderful place to learn. Most media curricula are structured so that the basics of film or television production in all phases are presented to the student. It is then up to the student to choose the discipline that he or she finds most interesting and pursue it in a more specialized course. A good media department has the equipment necessary to provide a working knowledge of the technology. Best of all, each department has people who are paid to train you to use it.

The only fault that I find with the typical school curriculum when it comes to TV and film is that it is woefully short of training in a lot of areas that are important to the business. The most glaring omission is in the field of producing. Few colleges teach you how to organize the elements of a shoot, such as putting together a crew, pricing equipment, scouting locations, locating talent (actors and actresses), and synchronizing schedules. This doesn't mean that this type of experience is unavailable. Since all of the elements that I mentioned are crucial to any production, the first-time student trying to put together a production will learn quickly just how necessary organization is to production. And the first-timer will either love it or hate it. If he hates it, he will find somebody else willing to do it, and so learning to delegate crucial duties starts with the simplest shoot.

Since the talents of a producer are mostly unteachable, having to do with personality and sheer stamina, the college media department focuses on the technical aspects of production and postproduction. The most important method of teaching is *hands-on training*. Through a series of assignments that begin with the basics and become progressively more difficult, you will actually hold a camera in your hands, design lighting setups, and edit film and tape, and you will do it until you get it right.

No studio manager in his right mind would trust his equipment, which is worth thousands upon thousands of dollars, in the hands of a newcomer who has never wrapped a cable in his life. But if you can demonstrate a basic knowledge of the equipment in question, you are more likely to get a chance to use it on a job. College is a good place to get the feel of the equipment.

College also is a great place to make mistakes. I have yet to meet a student who ever got fired from college.

In school you are expected to make mistakes. One fellow I knew was shooting a movie on a sidewalk, and he had the camera screwed on tight to a tripod and the tripod anchored with sandbags. While he was taking a light meter reading a few feet away, a speeding bicyclist careened around the corner and smashed into the camera, tripod, and sandbags, sending the whole works into the shop for weeks. The head of the college film department tore his hair. The other students were both amused and angry, since that left one less camera for them to share. And the student learned that he *always* should have someone standing next to the camera. If he had been working for a news team, the shoot would have been ruined, the newscaster enraged, the station out a lot of money, and the cameraman looking for work, dragging his clumsy reputation behind him. If you make those kinds of mistakes in school, you are likely to be given another chance. By the time you go looking for work, you'll have taken your lumps and can go into the business with a clean slate.

If you find TV or film equipment frightening or its function boring, remember that there is a lot more to the business than pointing cameras and snipping at scenes. An ambitious student who would like to organize a shoot can make herself or himself available to other students as a producer. And, of course, actors and actresses seeking experience can find a lot of it by acting in student productions. Because many student films are available on campus, clever distributors can get their feet wet in the business by putting together festivals. In the journalism department, which tackles different aspects of the field, courses are offered in news writing, directing, reporting, and all kinds of advertising. Many courses are available in marketing research and ad campaign design. In a college environment, all of these departments will work together to give the student an

THE TRAINING GROUND

idea of how the same departments work together in a competitive business environment.

The greatest advantage to learning the ropes in school is that the student works with peers who are at the same level of learning. Through the course of training, a few students will stand out and assume leadership roles. Those who emerge with what can be considered a successful track record are usually the students who genuinely want to work in television or film. By applying themselves and gaining important experience *outside* of the courses offered, the student is prepared to be equally diligent when he or she enters the work force.

Another advantage to training in college is that the student emerges from school with the classic "well-rounded education." That means, in video and film, that the student is at least familiar with every aspect of production, with knowledge that will be helpful when dealing with the people in positions outside of his discipline. In this business, every department relies on the other departments, and communicating with clients and bosses in a language that they understand is extremely helpful.

A crucial advantage goes to the students who go on to positions in the industry. Let's suppose that ten students out of a class of thirty go on to work in jobs all over the country, shooting, producing, or writing. At some point in the future, those students will rise to positions of influence and skill. At the same time, they are not only your peers, they are your former classmates, which is a bond not to be ignored. When the chips are down, you can look up an old friend who has started his own company.

The first disadvantage of training in college is that college is expensive. But many schools offer good programs at a reasonable price; they are listed in the

Appendix. Another disadvantage is that, despite the rising cost of college, many video programs do not see that extra money funneling into their department. As a result, a lot of schools are stocked with obsolete equipment. Add this to the incredible amount of use that the equipment gets from all of the students in each course, year after year, and you often find film and TV departments that have little to offer but outdated, broken equipment. You may get a great lesson in patience and resourcefulness, but in the long run you have to become familiar with the equipment that is in use in the industry. When looking for a school that suits you, find out what kind of equipment is available and what shape it is in.

The final disadvantage is that there is no substitute for experience in the industry. It is difficult to obtain the education that day-to-day work provides. That is why I recommend that the serious student supplement his or her education with extracurricular experience that other local facilities provide.

CABLE ACCESS STUDIOS

Public access programming accounts for one or two channels of the many offered by local cable companies. That is because the cable industry is required by law to provide studio and equipment access to the public to satisfy public interest requirements. While a cable service provides movies, educational programs, reruns, and so on, they also must provide facilities and air time to folks like you and me. If you have seen public access programs, you will agree that most of them look as if they have been put together by people who know little about television. That is true. But if you think about it, considering our traditionally passive approach to television, it is truly great that we can step in and become active participants.

The Training Ground

The important aspect of public access programming is not how it looks, but that ideas and issues that might not otherwise be seen on TV are now available to the willing viewer, and the presentation of those ideas is available to the interested producer.

The best thing about public access is that it is free. Most access studios do not charge for their services. The same goes for air time, except in very large markets where the cost of airing a show is still cheap by any standards. The standing rule is that anybody can use the facilities, provided they learn how to use them! The people who run these places are like the studio manager who looks with horror on the inexperienced lout manhandling his camera. But they still have to provide the access. What do they do? They can make sure of this by teaching you. Once you've attended a required number of their training sessions, the mystery of video technology will vanish and you'll be shooting your very own program. Or, if you prefer, they will provide someone to help you with your project.

In my mind, that has to be one of the greatest offers ever made. All you have to provide is the time and your attention, and you're on your way to making major motion pictures. But aside from the selfish pleasures, this kind of system has some genuine benefits. For example, community groups who have no interest in beginning or furthering a career in video can generate many beneficial programs that you would never see on commercial television.

One example is a youth group for troubled kids in Iowa City. These children, ages ten to fifteen years old, organized a production team, wrote their own script, shot their own video, cut it, and showed it on the air. The result was some refreshingly honest and fun-loving footage that beats anything I've seen during prime time. The same goes for senior citizens' groups that use the access for news programs, health shows, and entertainment for older adults. I spent my free time at college training these people to use the equipment and helped them through their first programs. When they knew enough to go it alone, they threw together some great stuff that I will always remember.

However, there are also some very specific disadvantages to this type of training. The least of them is the fact that, while training you in the use of their equipment, the access studio provides little or no artistic training. As to style, rules of the game, pacing, lighting, and every other creative choice, you're on your own. Of course, if they did provide such glamorous ideas all the programs would look the same. So they leave the producers to their own devices and hope for the best they can get in twenty-eight minutes.

Although cable access studios are happy to train people to use the equipment, that equipment is generally less than state-of-the-art and suffers the wear and tear that is expected of overused equipment. On top of that, because of the demand for the equipment and the large size of the training sessions, the training is rudimentary. You will learn the bare essentials of operating the equipment, and the cable producer working in the field often must learn the limitations of the equipment while shooting on location. Again, patience and resourcefulness are necessary in this kind of situation.

The biggest disadvantage to working with public access facilities is the stiff competition for time. A lot of people want to take advantage of the opportunities provided by the system. The result is that equipment and studio time and post-production facilities are heavily booked and you have to fit yourself and your project into a tight schedule. Because of that, you won't often

THE TRAINING GROUND

get the time that is really required to produce a program of quality, or you'll have to wait a while before you get to work at all. That is particularly frustrating when you want to record an event that you could well miss shooting because of scheduling conflicts.

That is why I believe that neither college training nor public access training is enough in itself to give you the kind of experience you need to get a respectable background in video production. But together, these two training grounds work very well and can give you the blend of academic training and professional experience that will prepare you for a start in the video industry.

LOCAL TELEVISION STATIONS

When I referred to public access experience as "professional" I was stretching the definition. In terms of meeting deadlines and seeing a finished program of yours make it on the air, the experience meets professional standards. But in reality, until you are paid to work in the video industry you are not a professional, and many prospective employers will remind you of that. There is nothing like the credibility of getting paid to do what you want to do. And there is nothing like working with a professional team to put you on a par with other professionals. A job with a local television station can add a lot of weight to your résumé, and will be more beneficial than any amount of academic training.

Many local television stations offer internships in nearly every department. You must apply to the station for an internship, much as you would apply to get into a school, and the number of internships is limited. But the experience you can gain as an intern is very valuable. You'll work with professionals who know things about the business that a professor wouldn't dare tell you. These people usually are staff members who work in video for a living, which is what you want to do. Most of them will be what I call Happy Givers—more than willing to impart their knowledge to you, for a variety of reasons. First of all, when a youngster becomes fascinated with a job that one woman has been doing for twenty years, it refreshes the professional and gives her the chance to rediscover her trade, which might have become repetitive after so many years.

A different type of professional will do his best to discourage you by griping continually about the business. You have to watch out for the Griping Professional, because he will try to scare you with tales of poverty and forty-hour days in the same breath until you are convinced that the only people who work with video can't find an honorable line of work. That's not true. What the Griping Professional is trying to tell you is that he adores his work and wouldn't give it up for the world, and if anybody finds that out he might have to work for nothing. It's his way of keeping guilty pleasure to himself.

Another type you might run into as an intern is the employee who ignores you. He or she is trying to get a job done, a good job, a professional job, and you're just in the way with your tireless questions. The best thing to do with that type is leave them alone. Work hard and stay out of the way, and one day you'll get a compliment from this Ignorer, and that compliment will be far more rewarding than any from the Happy Giver or the Griper.

What's really nice about an internship at a local television station is that, if you do a good job, you have a good chance of landing a paying job at the same station once the internship is over. First of all, the station has spent some time training you for a particular job. Let's say you've been an intern cameraman for three months.

The Training Ground

During that time, you have become familiar with the studio cameras by working the six o'clock news. After three months of half-hour newscasts, you have a good working knowledge of the studio system. After a month or so you can anticipate the director and take more responsibility for camera moves. You make fewer mistakes. At the end of the internship, the studio has to make a decision: they can bring in a new intern, whom they will have to train; they can hire a cameraman who doesn't know the ropes; or they can keep you because you can step right into the ranks. Chances are you'll be hired as a cameraman (assuming the studio needs one, and the studio is *always* looking for them), and you'll be moved to bigger duties, leaving room for a new intern whom they won't have to pay.

If the studio is not looking to hire anyone, you'll still be on top of their list when there is an opening, because they know your name and they know what you can do. The time spent as an intern is a good investment.

As you might expect, the rosy picture of the internship has a few glitches of its own. The one that should come as no surprise is that interns never get paid. That's what being an intern is all about. It is a basic equation that says you will work for nothing and in exchange the station will provide you with the gold bars of experience. Another way to put it is that the station gets a little free labor without putting out any extra effort toward your education, other than letting you on the floor and giving you a bit of responsibility. The rest is entirely up to you.

Don't think the station isn't aware of the bargain and won't take advantage of it. When we discuss the going rates for a cameraperson, you'll know why your free labor means big savings for the station. Since you'll be unfamiliar with the studio system at first, you'll spend some extra hours of training. Once you know what you're doing, the station will pencil you in for an enormous amount of hours (at no pay). You can expect at least twelve a day during normal procedures. If you happen to be working in a newsroom setup, you'll soon learn about the trials of journalism when a crisis breaks. It can be very exciting and grueling and, in a fraternal way, binding, and you can feel privileged because you were on top of the story before it was broadcast.

I was an intern at CBS in New York one summer, operating merely as a set of eyes and ears. I wasn't allowed to touch anything, and I wasn't supposed to pester people about their jobs while they were working. With my hands shoved deep into my pockets so I would not touch any equipment, I stood behind backdrops and leaned against the wall of the control booth, unnoticed and unobtrusive. It was there in the newsroom that a UPI printer ticked off a message from Israel that Prime Minister Menachem Begin had suffered a heart attack during a meeting of the legislature. The message read,

> Jerusalem.
> Menachem Begin has suffered an apparent heart attack and had to be helped from his seat and out of the Knesset. Stop.

This simple bulletin stopped the newsroom cold. The chief editor was called. Walter Cronkite, who was still the news anchorman at the time, joined the mob that stood around the UPI machine waiting for some sort of confirmation to print out before their eyes. Nothing else came. They didn't wait any longer. The chief editor mobilized the emergency broadcast booth and enlisted a reporter to sit there and wait for the story to break. Cameras were warmed up. Expensive satellite time was purchased so that CBS could broadcast an emergency feed to its affiliates. All network news agencies have a video file cabinet stocked with prepared obituaries of famous and important people who might breathe their last in the near future. These tapes are built on excerpts from brilliant career moments, famous crises, clips from interviews, and so on, and they are constantly updated. They are like video headstones waiting for the final date to be etched into the face of somebody's lifetime. Begin's tape was pulled and readied for the last entry. A control room was activated.

After two hours of anxious waiting, the UPI printer buzzed to life:

Jerusalem.
Begin suffering from indigestion. Stop.

Shelve the obituary. Cancel the satellite. Send the reporter home. Power down the camera. False alarm. CBS News returned to standard operating procedure.

Observations such as this are the rewards of an internship that allows the intern to look but not touch. But all of that looking can make the long hours of internship even longer, and one can only feel helpless and unproductive standing around while everybody else is working.

If you are lucky enough to get an internship that permits you to gain hands-on experience, you'll have to consider one more disadvantage to that route: lack of mobility. We know that the experience offered at schools and cable production facilities is varied and comprehensive, with little in-depth training available. The local TV station internship offers just the opposite. Your training and experience will be restricted to your chosen area. You will, in fact, learn just about everything there is to know about the job at hand, and lack only the long-range experience it takes to become an expert. But you must remember that the experience you gain at any particular job will pertain to that job and that job only. If you have taken an internship as an editor, for instance, you can forget about learning how to run a studio camera.

It is true that by focusing on one aspect of TV production (pre-, or post-), you are more likely to discover that you either love or hate your chosen area of expertise. But that can become frustrating if you get stuck doing something you don't want to do. Such a situation means loss of valuable training time and waste of an internship that wasn't easy to obtain. My advice is to be prepared for the restrictions of this kind of internship, be prepared to assume a position that you have researched and decided was the place you wanted to start; having done that, you will be prepared to reap the hearty benefits of the toughest and most extensive kind of training available in the video business.

I have introduced three possible training grounds for gaining good experience: universities and colleges, cable access studios, and local TV stations. All three take a certain amount of thought and sometimes money. The reason I chose them as the Big Three of TV is because examples of each training ground are near you, they are accessible, and everybody has an equal opportunity to learn and grow no matter where you go.

But there is another route that is restricted for two reasons: location and temperament. If you happen to live near a production company of some kind, you should try walking in the door and offering your soul to the employment office. Someone may have recently quit or retired or moved on and you might just be in the right place at the right time. It has happened before.

The Training Ground

If you are willing to accept a role as a "gopher," you will have made the all-important breakthrough of getting in the door. Once you are inside a facility and people get to know your face, there's no telling what can happen. If you don't live near a production facility, obviously this advice doesn't apply to you. And if you don't have the temperament to become a slave with never-ending energy, the route is not for you either.

In some cases, no matter which route you choose, you might spend quite a lot of time in training, sweating bullets and absorbing everything and working around the clock, only to discover that they have hired a kid fresh out of school to assist a director who just happens to be the kid's uncle. That kind of thing happens everywhere, in every kind of business imaginable. We'd like to believe that talent and experience and loyalty mean everything in promotions and rewards, but they don't hold a candle to nepotism.

How can you deal with that kind of injustice, even if you are a born cynic? It's hard enough dealing with the justice. You make things happen and things happen to you. You might take one route and another will seem more expedient. You might take a route seems *too* expedient. The old Boy Scout motto says "Be Prepared," and I agree.

The trick is to have a general idea of what you want to do and where you want to do it. That will take some serious consideration of your goals and especially your attitude. What kind of person are you? Aggressive, quiet, hard-worker, manipulator, or malleable? There are jobs that best suit your personality, and there are enough jobs around to suit any type of personality, with some left over. But unless you have a personality that is split five ways, you have to face the fact that you can't do it all.

4

Name Your Poison

What I'm about to do is a lot like a card trick. Pretend that I'm holding a full deck and slowly, one by one, I drop cards in front of you. Stop me when you see your card.

Let's make it more interesting: Pick as many cards as you like. In fact, many cards work well together to form a royal flush of personal happiness and success. Anything is possible, but remember that selecting too many cards will only boggle your mind. And be aware that at any time in your career you can change cards, add cards, subtract, in fact, build a house of cards out of your experience.

In this chapter I'll describe the many positions available in video as best I can, and some are sure to appeal to you. Factor your goals and your attitude, and you narrow the choice. Since most of my examples have been related to technical production in video, we'll start with the nontechnical career positions that are available to you. Once you get an overall view of the kind of work that goes into the formulation of a production on any level, you will better understand how and when the technical end comes into the picture.

NONTECHNICAL PRODUCTION
Producer
If it were possible for one man or woman to do it all, he or she would be the producer. That is because the

producer is responsible for each and every phase of production, from the original idea to the actual production to the postproduction to the distribution and sales, right on down to signing of checks. In the case of studios that hire producers, the studio signs the checks. The producer is responsible for everything else.

The producer starts with a script or an outline of the project at hand. Usually she is sitting at home or in an office with a sheet of paper that describes the project, and immediately the producer gets a headache. Why? Because whatever is staring her in the face, whether it is a movie or a talk show or a documentary or an industrial or a commercial or a public service announcement or a community program, *it's going to cost money*, and plenty of it. The producer has to find the money. She'll call all of her rich friends. She'll submit umpteen grant proposals, search for challenge grants, query the corporations, apply for loans, empty her savings account, sell her car, anything, anything at all, until she has the money that this budget requires. Once the money has been gathered, the producer gets another raging headache. Why? *Because now she has to spend it*, every last nickel. And when the money is gone, there had better be a good show in its place.

A good producer has a million contacts in the business, and those contacts come from working in the business for a long time. Now is the time to call them up. Whom does she call first? Whom would you call if you had to put together a preproduction crew consisting of writers, researchers, production managers, talent coordinators, art directors, and all manner of specialists? If I were you, I'd call an assistant producer.

Assistant Producer

The assistant producer is the one who doesn't know how good he has it. He has every bit as much responsibility as the producer, except for the final blame and the worst headaches. The assistant producer takes over a lot of the paperwork and the hiring and the other, more tedious tasks so that the producer can be free to cope with the project as a whole. Because of this, the assistant producer is invaluable but invisible and gets noticed only when a mistake is made. There is not a lot of glory, but there is some power, and there is the knowledge that the next step is right up to producer.

The assistant producer handles the bulk of the one-on-one communications with the assistant directors, the budget department, and the rest of the people who head their respective jobs. Again, the key function is to free the producer so that she doesn't have to deal with day-to-day operations. The producer would much rather deal with the one person who can make or break the production.

Director
You hear an awful lot about directors. Some are tyrants, others pushovers; some are decisive, others waste time and money worrying about the weather—the list goes on. Before you decide that directing is your destiny and megaphones are your favorite mode of communication, you must realize that film directing and video directing are two distinctly different animals. The film directors are the Hollywood and Big Apple guys making major motion pictures and slick commercials and made-for-TV movies. Their names are biggest in the credits (beneath the producer).

The responsibilities of the video director are vastly different. In the studio, for example, the director calls the shots as the technical director punches up the selected camera or cameras. He has to direct not one camera, but often three or four at once, "on the fly," making split-second decisions and calling for effects that, in film, only the laboratory can produce. The video director works under an extremely tight time schedule, required to bring a program to completion right down to the exact second. That is because the demands of television programming are so precise. In many cases, the director has to do this live, which is no easy feat.

A documentary was made about the man who directs the Miss America pageant, which is a big, glitzy extravaganza. The director coordinated half a dozen cameras, countless song and dance numbers, music cues, lighting cues, prompters for the emcee, all measured to the last second so that the commercials could air on time and the show could continue on time after each of the numerous breaks. After weeks of preproduction, choreography, stage blocking, lighting corrections, last-minute changes, and synchronization of the technicians (at least one hundred), the show was about to go on the air live to millions of viewers. The director sat in the dark booth, the curtains poised to open, the orchestra waiting for the drop of the baton. As the assistant director counted off the last ten seconds to air time, the director leaned forward, his pen in the air, and said, "I don't want to do this."

For the broadcast video director, the rewards of such a production are like the rewards of a newspaper editor: After the mad scramble to meet a deadline, the product hits the streets and its life is over immediately, consumed and disposed of, discarded by the absent-minded public who wait impatiently for the next edition.

The commercial director has the consolation of knowing that his work will be repeated for a short while and that a successful commercial can mean a lot to his career. Video directors who work in the industrial or corporate training field have as many technical demands to meet, but not nearly the pressures of live broadcast.

In nearly every case, the director shares a great deal of the responsibility with the client, since the client provides the copy and, in some cases, the talent.

In community video production there is no director, and that leads to a more relaxed, personalized type of production. A case can be made that some of them could benefit from a director, but that sort of criticism doesn't apply to community projects. If you have to name a director in such cases, it would be the one who sees to it that all of the technical demands are met and that the equipment doesn't get trashed.

Ironically, the lack of a director in these circumstances illuminates one of the basic functions of a director in productions that utilize one: The video director is really a guide, an authoritarian who has both creative abilities and an analytical mind. Those are the two greatest assets of the video director. The creative ability allows the director to see every aspect of a production from a creative angle, such as the compositions, lighting, hairdos, anything that will affect perception of the program. The authoritarian aspect encourages the crew to respect those creative views, and the analytical mind allows the director to make critical decisions about creative matters while under a great deal of pressure. And the director is *always* under a great deal of pressure. The test of a director is how his conviction stands up over the course of a production, whether his own energy level is maintained, whether he can maintain the energy on the set under grueling conditions, and whether he can satisfy both the demands of the client and the demands of his own creative desires. If the balance between client demands and creative demands is shaken, the product often suffers and so does the director. He's walking a tightrope at all times, and for all of the assistants and onlookers standing beneath him, not one will be able to break his fall.

NAME YOUR POISON

The video director can prevent such calamities from happening. The best way is to cover all of the angles during preproduction. The director is involved with the production from the very start, breaking down the script into a shooting script, making corrections, blocking positions for both the camera and the talent, planning the production so that it will be as simple as possible and therefore make postproduction editing equally simple. Every second of production time is accounted for. Efficiency is the name of the game. A good video director makes sure that the actual production goes like clockwork. If there is a problem of any kind, which often happens, the director is prepared with an alternate plan, one that can be implemented without loss of time. To insure that the demands of the clock are met, the director has at his side an irreplaceable assistant.

Assistant Director
In a film production, the assistant director is actually an extension of the producer and acts very much like video's assistant producer. But in video the assistant director is married to a stopwatch. The assistant director, or AD, must have one eye glued to a stopwatch at all times. During preproduction it is the AD's responsibility to see that the time allotted for each section of the program is given a specific time, and that each section adds up to the required total time. In a nonbroadcast production, the AD has an easier job of it and works more directly with the director as a right arm and as a liaison with the production staff. But in a broadcast situation, the AD sits in the booth with the director, stopwatch in hand. The AD knows *exactly* how the production should move and calls out directions to the director at least ten seconds before he is supposed to call the same direction. It is interesting that the AD can look into the face of a stopwatch and, beneath the sweep

of the second hand, see the video production taking place without looking at a television screen. The AD is the voice of the director, speaking before the director speaks so that not only will the director be prepared for his next move, but the remainder of the crew in the booth will be ready to excecute that move.

The service of the AD is extremely important to the production because the AD provides the structure and the boundaries of the production. The discipline and concentration the job requires are an important element in the development of the AD into a full-fledged director.

Line Producer (Talent Coordinator)

Many nontechnical jobs exist in the production office that have a lot to do with what goes on the television screen. If you have ever watched a talk show, you have appreciated the work of a line producer without even knowing it.

The line producer's job is to locate and secure the people who appear on interview and magazine shows all over the airwaves. Most shows of this type are flooded with promotional releases and invitations to invite someone onto the program. The daily talk show is an ideal promotional tool for any entertainer or inventor or publicity-seeking type, and so the line producer has to find those characters who will actually be interesting once they are on the air. The real trick of the line producer is not to find one interesting character, but to put together a blend of talent that should benefit from good chemistry during an interview. If the line producer picks a few duds who freeze the instant the red light goes on over the camera, the line producer is going to hear about it from the host, who looks bad on camera and won't like that one little bit.

Line producing entails a lot of telephone work and follow-up calls to make sure that the talent gets to the set in plenty of time, but there are some nice advantages. For instance, it is the line producer who is supposed to meet with the guest and make sure he or she is happy. Often that will be a movie star or a famous author, and it is possible for the line producer to develop a working relationship with very creative and successful people. When it comes time to move on to other things, assuming that the line producer doesn't go on to become a producer within the same organization, those contacts can come in very handy.

Researcher
This job is exactly what it sounds like: Find out as much as you can about someone or something, put it all together in a neat bundle, and give it to somebody else to work with. In some ways it is a lot like writing a term paper for pay. In other ways it's a lot like investigative reporting, which sounds more exciting. Either way, it takes a good mind for facts and details and a relentless search for pertinent information.

When you watch a show like "60 Minutes," keep in mind that nearly all of the leg work and real investigation have taken place long before anyone steps in front of the camera. The researchers are the real heroes of that successful program. The researcher sifts through all the possible angles for shows that have been provided by folks from all over the country who want their story told, and also from alert producers who spot a story that might be worth investigating. The researcher does the initial investigation, finding out all there is to the story, sometimes traveling to the location to talk with the participants, performing the initial interviews, and presenting the producer with a comprehensive package.

The producers and the editors select the story that they want to tackle, and finally the on-camera host is given the package to develop. When the research has been handled well, nothing has been left out, and the reporter is pleased that his job has been made that much easier.

The job of a researcher is serious and without glory. It's a behind-the-scenes job and can be very rewarding when an investigated piece results in concrete action and sometimes justice. Celebrity reporters come to expect expert results from the experienced researcher, and often the reporter works with that researcher again and again, knowing that he can trust the research and that the research can only make him look better when the cameras roll. For a reporter who wants nothing to do with lights, makeup, and cameras, research is the ideal job.

The researcher also plays an important part in interview programs, but the job overlaps with that of the line producer. The difference is that once the guests have been selected, the researcher looks over the issues and formulates possible questions that the host can exploit during the interview.

The researcher really flexes his muscles when the project at hand is a documentary. Documentaries demand a great deal of information as well as a complete grasp of the issues. A good researcher is extremely valuable to the documentary because he can save the production a lot of money by doing good work in the library. The researcher spends long hours poring over microfilm, scrutinizing past newspaper accounts, digging up names and places, crucial dates, anecdotes, and as many skeletons in closets as can be found. After months of this type of investigation, the material is presented to the production staff and the writer; the unimportant material is discarded, the marginal information is shelved, and the meat of the story is laid out in a shooting script. By the time the equipment is rented and the crew is plugging in lights, the difficult task of the documentarian, finding what is important to a story, is simplified. Like the AD who can see a TV show in the face of a stopwatch, the researcher draws the documentary on a paper outline months before the program goes into production. The documentary is nothing without the wealth of information that the researcher provides.

Writer

Writers, writers, writers: They are everywhere. In offices, at home, in the corner booth at the coffee shop, on a stool in a saloon, on the beaches, in the basement, everywhere and anywhere they scribble and type. I can't think of a single type of video production that doesn't need a writer to make it happen.

Since there are so many ways in which a writer can assist a video production, we'll start with the very beginnings.

The first step from an idea into a production is the writing of a treatment. A treatment is a brief outline of the project that can be anywhere from one page to forty pages. It is designed to generate interest in a project so that potential investors will get excited and write blank checks to the producer. It is obvious that a good writer with a talent for making car repair sound absolutely thrilling can be a great asset to a producer. A poorly written treatment will sink a project in no time at all.

An offshoot of the treatment is the proposal, which is more specific in content and a lot less flashy. Proposals are intended to be seen by institutions that often provide grants to producers. Because of the formality involved in such a process, the proposal must be clearly presented as to intent, existing research, personnel descriptions, budget requirements, proposed shooting schedule, and financial backing available from other sources. Writing a proposal is a highly refined skill, and it is well known in the business that an excellent proposal writer can give you an excellent chance of seeing your project realized. Many writers who have perfected the skill make a living doing that and nothing else. A proposal writer is extremely valuable and always in demand.

Once the project has been accepted and funding provided, other kinds of writers are brought into the fold, depending on the nature of the project. Every narrative needs a scriptwriter. Even if the project is an improvisational number, there must be a framework from which the actors can work. Writing a script is incredibly tricky and often frustrating. First of all, the scriptwriter must use the terminology of the screenplay, which includes camera moves, scene changes, and some directional instruction in addition to strict page format for the separation of scene descriptions from character dialog. Any producer with a meager amount of experience reading screenplays will spot one written incorrectly and will immediately discard the script. But if you follow the technical rules and add the stylistic touches that can flesh out a good script, the rewards of seeing your work flickering across the screen are immeasurable. The pay is usually very good, and it is nice to know that a production came from your script.

The industrial script is very similar to the narrative script, with a few exceptions. Many industrial videos copy the format of the narrative so that the viewers, who are generally employees of the same firm, will relax and be more receptive to the message. The narrative structure is familiar to anybody who has ever watched television, and it kindles the imagination of the viewer. With this strong advantage, the industrial video can project its message of safety, sales technique, or efficiency advice to an audience that is more likely to respond to the familiar structure of the narrative. For the writer, it is a matter of inserting the client's message into the story and the dialogue, in place of what might seem like more naturalistic dialogue. For example, I was editing a tape for an insurance company that was training its salespeople to present its products. The first scene ended with the agent trying to close a deal with a young couple by requesting a check immediately. As you might expect, the young couple balked, resisted, and were angered by the agent's tactics. The agent immediately retreated, stumbling for reassuring words, and was thoroughly browbeaten by the young husband. That is clearly the wrong way to sell insurance. So what happens? The scene begins again, but this time the ending has been rewritten, with the sales agent confident and persuasive, the young couple convinced, and fade-out on the husband signing on the dotted line.

For the industrial video writer, this episode must be written twice: once for reality and once for the company. It is a good example of the kind of manipulation a writer must do to make the words in the characters' mouths ring true for both the viewer and the insurance company. It reminds me of the predicament of the director who walks the tightrope, struggling to maintain his balance. The writer must do the same thing, and if the script comes out imbalanced, the director's job on the set is that much harder.

Related to this kind of industrial writing is the writing of narration. Many industrials require a voice speaking over a picture, explaining what is going on in the simplest terms imaginable. Upon viewing, it looks as though the voice-over had been added to match the picture. In reality, the voice-over was written first, since the client can visualize the picture from the words, and then the director makes sure that the pictures he gets on tape match both the voice-over and the client's visualization.

Commercial writers can have a little more fun, but they have much less time to have it. There are all sorts of formulas for what are called "copywriters" to use when writing a thirty-second spot. One formula says to utilize seven beats per sentence for maximum audience perception. Another recommends repeating the client's name as often as possible. Either way, copywriting can be either drudgery or a thrill a minute, and with the short length of commercial spots, you can be sure that a new project will come your way every day.

The advertising agency is the copywriter's turf. If you want to be a copywriter, go there. Generally, the copywriter is given a few accounts to handle and occasionally update. If you can write coherently, and if you have some clever ideas for catch phrases and hooks, the job can be yours with little or no training. A creative mind is really what they want. And the copywriter is involved through every phase of production, which means you'll get to go on location for the shoots and be there when the spot is edited for broadcast. On smaller accounts, you may be able to produce a commercial or two. With a little imagination, the copywriter can move up to many desirable positions in the advertising business.

The industrial writer's guidelines apply to writers who work in educational videos and documentaries. In both cases, the emphasis is on voice-over narration. There is nothing worse than confusing narration, so the educational and documentary writer must have a solid grasp of his subject and make it interesting at the same time. That is no easy feat, and it is why good writers of this kind get more work in the business than they can handle.

Name Your Poison

In any and all phases of video production, it is the writer who provides the concrete foundation upon which the production is built. But do not believe that the writer has any tremendous control. The producer and the director are really in charge, and scripts are always subject to their desires. Script changes are a given in the business, and often they are made without consulting the writer. It's no big deal. And since there are so many writers around, it is never too difficult to fire one and find another on short notice. But if writing is your own burning desire, the plentiful opportunities in the video business are a gold mine for the ambitious scribe.

Script Supervisor

The script supervisor works on the set during production. Her job is to make sure that nothing in the script is left out of the production. The script supervisor stays with the director, as close to the talent as possible. If the talent flubs a line, it is the script supervisor's job to prompt the talent. This person is a great asset to the director, who hardly has time to scour the shooting script during production. The script supervisor tells the director how many pages have been shot, for example, and how many pages must be shot that day. She also knows the order of the shooting schedule, since taped productions are seldom shot in sequence and the order can be confusing. In many ways, the script supervisor knows the script better than the writer, since she has to be aware of how every line is to be shot and what will be shot next. The job leads the script supervisor to a position as an assistant director.

Art Director

An art director is really a luxury that comes with the more pricey production. Few companies can afford one, and fewer can afford the kinds of additions that an art director brings to the set. He is usually associated with feature-length movies, but in some cases an art director is brought into a video production.

More often than not, a major video production brings an art director onto the set to dress it and oversee the details. The kinds of details addressed are costumes, set decor, lighting, anything that has to do with the "look" of a production. It's a little like bringing in a decorator to redo your home, except that he also decorates your body, your face, the lights, the whole works. That is not to say that the art director actually does the work. Prop people, costumers, makeup artists, and set designers handle the hands-on labor. The art director's job is to get together with the director and come up with an overall design that will give the production a consistent tone. Once that has been decided, the rest of the crew gets down to work.

It is well known that advertising agencies are crawling with art directors. Any television commercial has three or four of them on the job, which means that all of them have to agree on the look. If you can afford it, an art director is very handy to have around, since most directors don't want to fool with the endless details that must be taken care of on the set or on location. As a profession, art directing can be very satisfying, since you are responsible for virtually everything that goes onto the screen, right down to the doorknobs. A background in design is helpful toward landing this type of job, as well as having what can be considered "good taste."

Production Manager

This is a tough job. It is just what it sounds like. If you have any idea what it takes to mount even the smallest production, you can guess how hard it must be to manage one.

When the assistant producer goes to work for the producer, hiring the key preproduction personnel, one of the first people she hires is the production manager, or PM. Many assistant producers have their favorite production managers, and they hire the dependable PM whenever there is a choice. That is because the PM is a workhorse with a tremendous memory for detail. Once the PM has been hired, the assistant producer can forget about hiring the crew. Most experienced PMs have a long list of technicians and nontechnical people, and the first thing the PM does is get on the phone and find out who is available. She can do this with a rough shooting schedule. But when it comes down to confirming the appointments, the PM had better have an exact shooting schedule mapped out. That means putting together a strip-chart that nails down everyone and everything to their exact time and place. This chart is a lot like a flow chart that you might use in science class. It begins with a list of all the actors, from the lead down to the last extra. The strip-chart lists their names, addresses, and phone numbers, including agents' numbers and answering services. An actor must be able to be located under any circumstances. Next to the actor's name on the chart are the days that he or she will be needed on the set. The PM puts actors and actresses together in a cluster on the chart according to the days they will be working. The idea is to avoid having an actor on the set on the first day of shooting and then bringing him or her back five days later for another scene. The PM wants to shoot every scene with Actor X at one time, so that he or she can work the three or four days and be finished. That permits the actor to go on to other work, go out of town, get a haircut—all the things he or she cannot do during shooting.

That doesn't sound so tough when you think of only one actor's role, but it gets more complicated with the many performers needed for a production. The same kind of schedule must be charted for everyone. The real chore is to coordinate the schedule so that it works for every actor, eliminating the chances for complications and maximizing efficiency. You may need actors, A, B, D, and F for day one, A, F, and R for day two, A and R for day three, and so on.

The amount of time for which you need the actors depends upon the number of scenes that can be shot in a given day. So the next section of the chart lists the scenes to be shot on that day. (The average is two scenes per day, depending on the number of camera setups.) This part of the chart includes the script pages for each scene, so that each actor is prepared for the scene. The PM also indicates the nature of the scene on the chart. Is it an interior or an exterior? A morning shot? Nighttime scene? All of those variables must be accounted for. What if the scene is an exterior in the park, a beautiful autumn day, and it rains? The production manager must be prepared for a "rain day" with an alternate location that can be shot indoors without loss of time or money. If you've got ten thousand dollars worth of equipment and crew rented for the day, and you can't change the script from sunny autumn to torrential rains, somebody is out a lot of money, and the production manager is in a lot of trouble.

Maybe that doesn't sound so tough, running around with a camera and some actors, looking for a place to shoot. But consider this: For every location (approximately sixty for a narrative program), the production must have a permit from the city, permission to shoot, or a reservation at a studio. You can't just shoot anywhere you please. The PM must secure the locations in advance and, above all, see to it that everybody involved in the production gets to the same place at the same time. Anyone who has ever tried to put together a weekend softball game knows how difficult it is to get everybody together. Multiply that experience one hundred times and put thousands of dollars on the line, and you get the picture.

Okay, so the production manager gets the crew and the actors to arrive in the park at 6 A.M. for a morning shoot. What's next? Coffee! Actors and crew *must have coffee*! After all, 6 A.M. is pretty early. You have no idea how crucial this is to the sanity of everybody involved in a production. They simply must have a vat of steaming coffee waiting for them in the middle of the park at six in the morning. And the director drinks tea! The cameraman won't touch anything but Perrier water! Your star can't perform without eating a stack of flapjacks in the morning! If you wait until that fateful morning to find these things out, it's too late. The crew will be grumpy, and it will show on the screen. But if the PM knows all of the idiosyncrasies in advance and is prepared for them with a table spread with everybody's wishes, you'll see the happiest, most cooperative crew that ever laid down a take, and they'll love you for it! A little foresight and a good memory can make the production manager's job a lot easier, and that goes for the director, too.

The same goes for all of the magnificent details that the art director has ordered for a particular scene. If an art director has been hired to fluff the set, the stuffing had better be there or you've wasted the art director's time and the producer's money. The list of things that cannot be forgotten is unimaginable, but it might include mittens, tongue depressors, spare shoes, cold lasagna, eight tiny reindeer, two sledgehammers, one new and one broken, a wig, and a newspaper from 1929. Not only does the PM have to find these things, but she must make absolutely sure that they make it on the set or on location when they are needed, that they are obtained for free, and that if they are to be returned, they return in better shape than they arrived. If the tongue depressors are an absolute must for the scene, the PM will see to it that there are boxes of them on the set, or everybody loses. I repeat: There are many PMs who could find all of these things and get them where they belong, but the production manager who gets them for free is the one who will find more work. That takes a very special persuasion that few PMs have, much less the rest of us. But those who do have that special talent are tailor-made for the production manager's trade.

It should be obvious that the scenario I have presented is probably more difficult than it would really be. But as a production manager you have to expect the worst, because the worst is always happening. There are some situations, however, where the worst is less likely to happen.

In the studio, every member of the crew has more control over his or her task. The production manager delights in working at a studio for several reasons: no rain, no airplanes overhead or subways underneath to spoil the sound. The lights can be left hanging, the set can remain standing, there is no need for permits, no need for police, little need to worry. Location shooting can be a nightmare, but studio shoots make life bearable. The PM still has all the responsibilities mentioned before, including coffee and lunch, but when you work at a fixed location for any length of time those details can be taken care of in a routine manner. It is much easier to make the call for the next day, since you have only to announce the times people are expected on the set. Props can be stored without being lost, phones are readily available, and backup equipment is always at your disposal.

In the video business, you are more likely to be working in the studio. If you're working in the field, the situation will probably be much smaller and less complicated than the one I described. The production manager is not considered a luxury, since not having one means that somebody, probably the producer or the director, has to spend time on details that take concentration away from the task at hand. But many small-scale video productions cannot afford a production manager because the job is a nontechnical one. Some productions keep their crews as lean as possible, hiring only technical personnel and a director and leaving the PM's task to the producer, who wishes he had secured more money for the production so that he didn't have to worry about that stuff.

The important thing to remember is that most productions that don't have a PM wish they had one, and those that do are glad. For my money, the production manager has the toughest job of anybody involved in production. It's a lot like being a drill sergeant in charge of a platoon. The producer is the commander in chief and the director is the general, but the enlisted men and women look to their sergeant for immediate guidance. You must have a special temperament to handle a mountain of details, coordinate countless elements, and succeed in dealing with a team of professionals with a rainbow of personalities.

Production Assistant
The production assistant is a beginner who is generally referred to as a PA. It is an entry-level job much like the "gopher" I referred to earlier.

The PA is directly responsible to the production manager, and because of that he is indispensable on a production of any size. Because the PM has so many responsibilities of her own, the PA is called upon to carry out many of those duties. Most productions hire two PAs because one is always running around looking for something, and one should always be on the set.

What are the duties of a PA? You name it. The PA runs out for coffee, picks up lunch and forgotten equipment, helps push the dolly and hang the lights, cleans the set, pulls nails, quiets crowds, cues crowds to yell, takes photos, makes all kinds of deliveries, and does everything as fast as possible. In reality, a production assistant is an able body that is available to do anything on or off the set. The more a PA can do, the more work he gets. It helps to be able to drive, especially manual-transmission vehicles, trucks and vans, and it helps to be strong. Loading and unloading heavy stuff is a primary function of the production assistant.

That doesn't sound so hot, does it? It could be worse. If you talk to anybody in the video *or* film business, at any level, chances are that he or she worked as a production assistant at one point or another. It falls under the heading of "paying your dues."

What are the benefits of being a PA? First of all, it gets you on the set or in the door. That is very, very important, because half of this business is meeting people. The break comes when somebody remembers you, and how can they remember you if they never saw you? A job as a PA gives you a chance to see how a set works, understand the chain of command, and plug into the pace of a production. A good PA learns to anticipate the needs of the crew and be there when needed. But it is important not to overstep your bounds and take responsibility away from the production manager. If you make the decisions that a PM should be making, it looks as if the PM is expendable, and that makes her look bad. Then you'll see just how disposable a PA can be. Poof! Gone. There are a lot of bodies available for positions as PAs, and you'd be amazed at how many people would kill for a job that pays little and demands so much.

Production assistants are generally film students in college or fresh out of college. They are hungry for that first job in the business and happy to get one. As a result, PAs work like dogs to please everybody so that the next job will come easier. There are so many of these eager beavers out there that finding the first PA job can be quite difficult. That is where contacts come in. Since there are literally hundreds of available PAs for every job, and since the job itself requires little or no experience in the video business, the production manager could choose a name from a hat and still get what she wanted in a PA. It is not the sort of job selection that takes a lot of thought. So when an acquaintance mentions someone who'd like to PA for a production, the PM is likely to agree to it because (1) it makes her job of hiring much simpler, and (2) if she hires this PA for her acquaintance, the acquaintance owes her a favor in the future.

I know that makes the PA look like a throwaway item, but in a way, he is. He is a miniscule cog in the works of a video production. But, because he is a cog at all, and because he frees someone else to concentrate on his or her own job, the PA is a necessary item. Also, since most video professionals have slaved in the same way during their career, there is a certain measure of respect mixed with sympathy for the production assistant. In many ways, becoming a PA on a video production is like joining a fraternity. Someday, when you've climbed your ladder, you'll be surrounded by fresh and eager production assistants, and you'll remember.

Set Designer

While we are on the subject of the set, let's take a look at the people who design it. The set designer works strictly in the studio and can be included as a luxury item in our list of nontechnical video assistants. Since the set designer doesn't work on location, half of the work in video production goes on without him. And since a lot of studio shoots make less than a cursory effort on the set, that leaves a lot less work to be done by the set designer.

When the production is something like a weekly series (talk show, cooking show) the set designer is brought on early to design a few possible choices for the set. Once a set has been chosen and the designer has supervised the construction, the set designer's job is done. His real task is to create an imaginative, inexpensive, efficient set that will look great on the TV camera. The interior of every TV show you've ever seen, from "The Honeymooners" to the "Tonight Show," benefits from a set that some designer spent grueling hours designing.

The nice bit about the job is that it translates easily from film to television to theater, so that the minimal work available in each medium is made up for in the adaptability of set designing. Also, set designers always have great-looking apartments.

Property Master

This is one of my favorite titles. To be called a master of anything is a great compliment, and there is the same kind of charm to the actual task of the property master, who is in charge of every inanimate object on the set.

The word "prop" derives from "property," and a prop is something that should always be in the right place. When you watch a TV show, especially a narrative, look for all of the props on the screen: a gun, a pack of cigarettes, a pencil, the books in the bookshelf, the blinds, the whole works. Each prop has a specific place and a specific person who puts it there. That is the property master.

In some cases, the property master is responsible for obtaining the props that are needed for a production. That can be a lot of fun, since it generally means hopping from one antique shop to another, looking for a tiny glass unicorn. The property master develops an attachment to these knickknacks and can become known for some rather unusual behavior. I remember in particular a property master we called Ben-wah. He was French, his background was in theater, and when he moved to the United States, he brought with him nothing but his collection of props that had become his friends over the years. His favorite was a mechanical monkey that banged together little brass cymbals when wound up. He called it his "clappeeng minky." On every set he ever worked on, he would plant the clapping minky in the background somewhere, for good luck. Any kind of show at all. His masterpiece was a corporate video for an investment firm that uses a brawny bull as its symbol. It's unlikely that you'll ever see the tape, since it was used exclusively for training purposes, but Ben-wah left his mark. There was a department chief sitting at his desk talking about mortgage loans, his walls covered with diplomas and merit achievements; behind him was a shelf full of imposing books, the honored statuette of the bull, and beside it Ben-wah's clapping monkey. It was the ultimate in French cymbalism.

Graphic Artist
The graphic artist works behind the scenes to create titles and pictures for industrials, promotional tapes, narratives, and especially news programs. When you

watch the news, look over the shoulder of the newscaster. For just about every story, there will be a drawing or a title hovering in a little box behind him, which refers to the story. Those are graphics that the artist has put together for the newscast. Since news is broadcast several times a day and stories are changed at the last minute, many graphics must cover each report. The graphic artist is kept very busy, and there doesn't seem to be anything that can replace his talents.

Graphic art requires artistic skill and is related to the training you might get in an art class, cutting and pasting, and toying with color dynamics and types of print, but the graphic artist must move fast. It is another one of the those behind-the-scenes jobs that are so important to the appearance of a program, yet are taken for granted.

Floor Manager

The floor manager works exclusively in the television studio. She functions as an extension of the director or the assistant director, connected by a set of headphones and an intercom system. The floor manager is in charge of operations on the studio floor, such as cueing the talent and keeping them informed about running time. She demands quiet on the set and listens through the headphones for instructions from the control booth. Then she guides the production through, using hand signals so as not to interfere with the audio.

Another task of the floor manager is pre- and post-studio operations. That means setting up the cameras, putting the set in place, seeing that the studio is sealed during shooting and that nothing interferes, and wrapping the set after the production. "Wrapping" a set means shutting everything down (cameras and lights), rolling up cable, putting everything back in place, and seeing to it that the set is clean and ready for the next production.

Floor managing is a good example of a nontechnical job for someone who wants to be in production without becoming involved in the technical aspects of video production. There are many jobs such as these, as you have seen, and there are more that I chose not to go into because they don't necessarily relate to video exclusively. By that I mean makeup artists, costumers, carpenters, and so on. In truth, many of the chores formerly restricted to theater translate into video production without a problem. Those who have worked in the theater at such jobs are making the switch because television pays so much better than the theater. But if your goals are of the technical kind, there is plenty of work for you to do.

TECHNICAL PRODUCTION
Technical Director

The technical director, or TD, is the person who controls the switcher in the control booth. The switcher is the control board that "takes" to the selected cameras on the studio floor, "wipes" between sources, "dissolves" between sources, and gets any special effects that might be called for underway. Usually the sources that are available to the TD through the switcher are the cameras, graphics, the character generator, and prepared videotapes; it depends upon the sophistication of the studio's equipment.

The technical director takes his commands from the director. The director sits in the control booth, next to the TD, watching the television monitors. The director tells the camera operators to set up a particular shot, then cues the TD to cut to the selected camera. Everything that goes onto the master broadcast tape gets there through the hands of the TD.

The technical director must have a complete knowledge of the particular switcher that he operates. That takes a lot of practice and experience, since you get only one opportunity to get the moves right during a live production. Cutting to the wrong camera or effect looks bad and can be fatal to the program. The director depends on the TD to execute his commands with precise timing. The TD is, in many ways, the hands of the director.

It is customary for the TD to repeat the commands that come to him from the director. If the director says "Stand by to cut to camera one," the TD might say, "Ready to take one." The director then says "Take one" and the TD uses the switcher to make the cut. He then waits for the next command, and the process is repeated.

The TD must always be alert when he's on the job, because he is directly responsible for the finished product. He must also be on the lookout for incorrect commands, such as cutting to a source that hasn't been cued. That happens frequently during a live production because of all of the frantic decisions being made in the control booth, and the TD must be prepared to make his own decision to provide an acceptable alternative while the problem is being corrected.

The TD seldom works on location, because switchers seldom are used in that kind of situation. When a switcher is taken on location, the setup in the field is likely to be a replica of the studio control booth, and the same rules apply.

Often the TD and the director are one and the same. That happens frequently on lower-budget productions, and many directors actually prefer to work that way if they are familiar with the switcher. It eliminates one link in the chain of command that could pose problems for a production. The director simply calls his own shots

NAME YOUR POISON

The basic Grass Valley switcher controls the flow of the video.

and makes the transitions himself. The director as TD is especially effective if you are "winging it" through a production without a script, since most of the control remains in the hands of one person.

Experience as a technical director is extremely valuable for someone who plans to go into directing or editing. You get a good sense of shot combinations and, if you work with a smart director, you learn a lot about pacing as well. Once you've pieced a television show together with your bare hands, so to speak, the mystery of video production is solved.

VTR Operator
A VTR is a video tape recorder/player, and the operator must know how to run one. That means you should be familiar with VHS, 3/4-inch, 1-inch, Betacam SP, D–1, D–2, and other digital playback sources.

The VTR operator has a very specialized job. In the studio, he rolls the tape that records the production and rolls the tapes that will be used as source material. This usually occurs during newscasts, when the newscaster introduces the lead story, for example. As the reporter says, "The winner of the Marathon crossed the finish line in his bare feet today, and Maureen Bisbee was there . . ." the director is hollering "Roll tape three," the TD is setting up to cut to VTR three, and the VTR operator is kicking the machine into gear. By the time the newscaster says "Bisbee was there," the tape is running full speed, and if it is timed properly, the TD will cut to VTR three just as the first picture of Maureen appears on the preview monitor. In a network television situation, there are about thirty VTRs in the basement, each with its own operator, each with its own tape with news bits, commercials, special reports, and so on.

Studio productions of a smaller scale generally have the VTRs right there in the control booth, and the operator sits there with his finger poised over the key buttons. When not rolling the machine, the VTR operator must keep a keen eye on the recorder to make sure it is recording. Nobody pays attention to the VTR operator during a production, but if someone slaves over a hectic program only to find that the VTR operator forgot to record any audio, he'll start giving him plenty of attention.

Many film productions use what is called a "video tap" system. A video tap is a little black-and-white TV camera mounted over the lens of the film camera. It allows the director, the clients, and the art directors to watch a take immediately after it has been shot, to see if it needs to be shot again for some reason. The video tap eliminates some of the guesswork of filmmaking and illustrates the beneficial relationship between film and video. And, of course, a VTR operator is needed to operate the equipment. It puts a little more pressure on the cameraman, but it takes a lot of pressure off the director, since he can send the clients and art directors into another room to watch the TV monitor while he does his work in relative peace. The VTR operator who can run a video tap has a good shot at a lot of freelance work in film productions.

VTR operation is not a particularly demanding job. If you can get into the networks and land a job as a VTR operator, you'll be paid a handsome sum for knowing exactly how to run a specific piece of equipment.

Boom Operator
The "boom" is a large trolley on heavy rubber tires that has a long telescopic pole with a microphone attached. The boom operator stands on top of the dolly and moves the microphone by using a reel like a fishing reel. It shortens or lengthens the boom, and it turns the microphone in every direction. A good boom operator knows how to angle the microphone so that it points to the desired source, because if it is aimed wrong, the sound will be wrong. Also, it is tricky to operate a boom without interfering with the lights and throwing awkward shadows on the set.

With the advent of small, wireless microphones, the boom operator has had less and less work in the studio. In the old days, every dramatic production had a boom operator who could follow the action with one microphone. Nowadays, you can plant a microphone on everybody in sight and mix the sound in the control room. Still, boom operators are working on soap operas and other major productions, as well as film productions. Instead of being a specialized career, however, boom operator is now an offshoot of the audio engineering department.

The audio engineer records some ambient street noise with a Sennheiser boom mic, mounted on a "fishpole."

Audio Engineer

The title "audio engineer" sounds a little technical because the title in the past was "soundman." With the advent of women in the video production business, many of them audio technicians, the word "soundman" has disappeared and has yet to be replaced by a generic title. Because the job has so many functions, I'll use "audioperson" as the rather unspecific title.

The first task of the audioperson is to select a microphone that suits the needs of the production. There are many kinds of microphones, from hand-held mics to shotgun mics to lavalier microphones. Hand-held mics are self-explanatory, and shotgun mics are long, slender microphones with a narrow pickup range. But the story of the lavalier is a little more complex. The original lavalier was a small microphone that was worn around the neck by a string and was used in newscasts and talk shows. It got its name from the lavaliere, a pendant on a chain worn by women. Today the lavalier is much smaller and lighter and can be worn like a tie clip. Most lavaliers are the size of a gumdrop, yet the sound is crisp and can match even the best shotgun microphone.

Once the audioperson has selected the proper mic, she must decide where to place it, or, in most cases, where to place several microphones. That depends upon the location, the movement of the talent (actors), and the camera placement. For instance, if the location is outdoors, she might select a shotgun mic to get a full-bodied sound. If it is a windy day, however, the mic would pick up a lot of wind noise that is impossible to eliminate with a sound equalizer. So the audioperson would choose a lavalier, because it is much closer to the talent's voice box and can be protected from the wind. But you have to hide the lavalier if you're working on a dramatic production, and that means slipping it under a shirt or jacket and running the wire underneath the clothes. This poses two problems: First of all, giving the talent a lavalier is like putting him on a leash; it restricts his movement. Second, when a mic is tucked into clothing, there is a good chance that the rustling of cloth that we usually pay no attention to will be amplified to sound as if the talent has a forest fire in his breast pocket. If the camera is placed far away from the talent, attaching the talent to a cable is impossible, as is putting a boom operator anywhere near the talent. In

The portable digital video camera, ready for action.

this case, the audioperson might select a wireless mic, which is a lavalier connected to the recorder via radio. This allows the talent free movement without any change in voice level, but it also presents the countless problems that arise when you are fooling with a radio frequency. The air is full of radio waves, and if any are on the same frequency as your radio microphone, as soon as you tune in your actor all you'll hear is Top 40 radio. There are many variables involved with microphone selection and placement, and the audioperson must be on top of things so that she gets the best sound possible.

In the controlled environment of the studio, the task is a little easier. Most video studios are soundproof and eliminate the annoying noises that can ruin an otherwise good performance. There is little problem with running cables, and the talent's movement is restricted by the studio itself.

Once the audioperson has selected the microphones and placed them accordingly, it is time to go into the audio booth and begin measuring sound levels for each particular source. Besides the feeds from the microphones, video productions employ prerecorded sources such as records, reel-to-reel tapes, cassette tapes, and audio from prepared videotapes. All of these levels must be set to match each other precisely, or one source will sound inordinately loud compared to another. Since no two people speak at exactly the same volume, it is important to set the microphone levels on the talent so that one person seems to be speaking as loud as the other.

Once that has been achieved, the voice checks are complete, and the prerecorded sources have been cued up, the audioperson sits at the mixing board and prepares to mix all of the sources together. This is a lot like running a radio program. The audioperson's eyes should be glued to the meters that measure the sound level going into the recorder and the meters that monitor the sound that is actually recorded. During the course of a production, the audioperson must open the mics in use and be careful to close the ones that are not in use, so that, while one person is explaining the state of the economy, we don't hear another muttering expletives under his breath. A great many of the infamous television bloopers are the result of an open microphone on a person who thought he was off the air.

When an audioperson is working on location, it is unlikely that she will have the benefit of a mixing board or wireless microphones, which are used less frequently than you might think, because of their unpredictability. The basic video crew, called an "ENG crew" (Electronic News Gathering), consists of a cameraperson, an audioperson, and a reporter. On this type of crew, the audioperson is recording right into the video deck through a single microphone. Sometimes the reporter holds his own microphone; at other times the audioperson must point a shotgun mic while monitoring the sound levels through headphones. The latter is the more common practice, and it entails a certain amount of coordination and concentration.

Audio is a very complex science. Every sound has its own particular frequency that can be measured on a graph. A graphic equalizer divides the sound into a series of bands that can be controlled by a knob or a sliding "pot." By using a graphic equalizer, the soundperson can eliminate unwanted interference by eliminating a band or boost the good audio to an acceptable level. It takes a keen ear and a thorough knowledge of the intricacies of sound recording. The best audio recordists can identify wavelengths by ear and determine the optimum levels in a flash. That takes a great deal of experience and know-how that can be obtained only through constant practice.

The drawback to being an audioperson is that sound is really taken for granted. Since video is a visual medium, audio takes a back seat to the picture on the screen. As a result, many video productions suffer from poor sound recording that can ruin a good picture. On the other hand, excellent soundtracks can make a mediocre picture seem fantastic. The more attention you pay to your soundtrack, the better off you'll be with your video production.

It has been said that television is just "illustrated radio." That description is very telling when you consider the importance of audio to a video production. The creative use of music, voice, and sound effects can work wonders for a show. If you turn the sound off while you're watching television, you'll see how badly it is needed. In my opinion, a good audioperson is like gold to a production and is absolutely irreplaceable.

Gaffer

The gaffer is responsible for the lighting of a video production. This is another essential, creative job that calls for technical wizardry and the eye of a painter.

To understand the importance of a gaffer, you have to go back to basics to understand that without illumination, you have no picture. The first responsibility of the gaffer is to get enough light on the set so that the cameras can see what is going on in front of them. If that were all that was needed for a video production, the gaffer could simply blast a few thousand watts of light on the set and holler, "Fire away!" In fact, that is exactly the style of lighting that you see on many of the poorest cable television productions: bright, flat faces, shadows all over the place, and irritating reflections. The reason goes back to what we said in Chapter 3 about cable productions. When the video producers heard that the video camera could see with very little light, they just plugged in whatever was available and started taping. Fortunately for the viewer, producers have begun to "see the light" and realize that if video is lit the way a film is lit, the quality of the image is improved dramatically.

There are two basic schools of lighting—the naturalistic school and the stylistic school—and they demand

Daylight spilling in through the window is plenty of illumination for video.

different kinds of light. Documentaries are invariably naturalistic because of the limitations of time and place. Narratives have the time to be a little more artistic, or "arty," depending on your point of view. A good gaffer can deliver either style in a whole range of degrees. That sort of skill comes with an understanding of the principles of light that can be obtained only through study, experience, and experimentation.

Our eyes can adjust to light levels and color shifts without our taking notice. The iris of the eye is continually opening and closing to compensate for the multitude of light shifts that we encounter every minute. But a camera has to be told how much light there is on a subject, and, more important, the camera tells us how much light is needed to see. Even a camera with an automatic iris adjusts to the brightest object within view, which means that if your subject is standing against the sky, which is tremendously bright, the iris will adjust for the sky and your subject will become nothing but a dark silhouette. That is the reason for a primary rule in television that you never dress your subject in white. A white shirt will reflect all kinds of light, and faces will be swallowed up.

The gaffer must operate with the camera's eye in mind. That entails a knowledge of which colors absorb light and which reflect light. Likewise, different kinds of surfaces reflect light in different ways. That goes for every kind of surface you can imagine: flat walls, water, stucco, tile, newspaper, wallpaper, paneling, and so on. A gaffer is aware of all of these qualities of light reflection and lights his set accordingly.

Another aspect of lighting is color "temperature." To a video camera, sunlight is blue, lamplight is yellow. The camera must be "balanced" to compensate for color temperature by tweaking what is called the "white balance." By setting a white card in the light that you want to use for shooting and pointing the camera at that white card, you can adjust the camera so that it reads the card as a pure white. By filtering the lens of the camera, you can ensure that everything that falls within your lighting scheme will assume its natural color.

There are a lot of tricks to getting the proper colors on the television screen. If you are shooting outside and you've filtered for daylight, you must be aware of the kind of day it is. A cloudy day will be bluer than a sunny day, since the daylight is bouncing off the clouds. If you are shooting indoors and the bulbs you are using are old, they will tend to look more yellow, or "warmer," than they would if they were fresh. There are other variables that the gaffer must be aware of to make a lighting scheme work.

The gaffer has a great many tools at his disposal: lights, gels, diffusion filters, barndoors, clamps, cables, stands, flags, and reflectors. The lights come in a wide range of wattages, or strengths. Barndoors are the flaps on the lights that keep light from spilling onto things that you don't want lit. Gels, filters, and flags are special attachments that permit the gaffer a variety of special effects. Cables and stands are necessities, and reflectors are used to fill in areas with soft light reflected from the sun or other sources. There are gaffers who have many more devices, and there are gaffers who scoff at special attachments. But there is one tool that no gaffer will be caught without: good, old-fashioned, wooden clothespins. They are essential for clamping gels and filters onto scalding-hot barndoors because they are cheap, effective, easy to use and remove, and they don't burn. With a pair of thick work gloves and a pocket full of clothespins, you could be on your way to gafferdom.

The toughest job for a gaffer is to go on location to an interior and set up to shoot in somebody's apartment, a laundromat, or a drugstore. He is usually working in a confined space with few electrical outlets and little or no ventilation. Remember, when you've got five thousand watts of light cooking in your living room, it can get hot in a hurry. All of the lights and lighting equipment must be brought in and set up out of the way, so there is room to place the cameras and move the performers.

And there is the additional problem that no gaffer can ignore: electricity. The gaffer has to know what sort of power the lighting scheme is going to demand from a particular location. This information is gathered during preproduction, when the gaffer visits the location and spends a lot of time in the basement, glaring at the fusebox. Your typical house or apartment can feed only so much power into a room, and the gaffer is limited to the restrictions of the fusebox. That means that a gaffer must have the knowledge of a full-fledged electrician. He will employ an equation that is the rule of thumb for lighting: one thousand watts takes ten amps of power. Most apartments are supplied with twenty to

NAME YOUR POISON

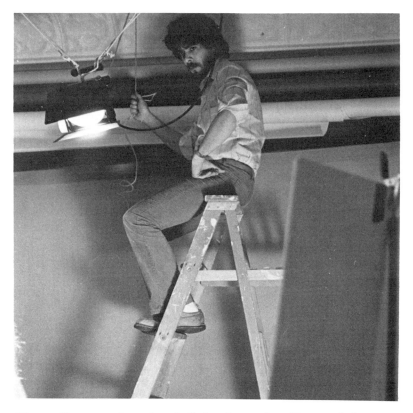

The gaffer tweaks a back light. A good gaffer can't have a fear of heights.

thirty amps, which means that the gaffer has to get by on two thousand watts of light or blow out all the fuses. This is a lot of information and skill that one technician must have in order to perform, and beyond that, he must be extremely creative.

Since film is more light-sensitive than video tape, experience at lighting for film is valuable to the gaffer who is lighting for video. With film, the gaffer does not have the benefit of a television monitor that he can consult to see how the light looks through the camera.

65

The gaffer uses a light meter when lighting for film, and the use of a light meter is instructional about the value and intensities of certain kinds of light. With a basic knowledge of lighting for film, the gaffer can use that information to light for video and get terrific results. Even though the video camera has some automatic abilities for exposures, and the TV monitor can show you exactly what you'll get on tape, I firmly believe that knowledge of film lighting is crucial to effective lighting for video.

In the old days, every news team shot its stories on 16 mm film. When that proved to be too expensive and slow, video tape was adopted by nearly every news organization in the country. There are a few holdouts, though. I remember a time when I was traveling with a news crew as an intern, and we took the van to a news conference and set up the camera. Every news team in New York City was there: the three major networks, including ourselves, local TV stations, and many independent crews. We were standing in a forest of tripods topped with video cameras. Alone among them was an old Arriflex film camera, looking forlorn, an endangered species among the new mutants. Somebody had thrown some lights onto the dais, and we were waiting patiently for the police commissioner to make his announcement. As we waited, one of the elder statesmen of cameramen walked up to the dais with a light meter, to measure the light so that he could set his exposure. He looked like a man with a geiger counter, waving it under the lights. There was a look of bemusement on the faces of the video camerapersons. The elder statesman held up his light meter for the crowd to see.

"Do you guys remember what this is for?" he said. Nobody did.

The point is that the elder statesman could chuck his Arriflex at any time, pick up a video camera, and be able to shoot in no time at all. But if one of those video cameramen were faced with the reverse situation, they'd be at a complete loss. So get that experience in lighting for film, and lighting for video will seem like a luxury.

Some gaffers know their craft so well that it's mind-boggling. Gordon Willis, the outstanding cinematographer who earned his stripes as a gaffer, was shooting a film called *Pennies From Heaven*. He was shooting in an enormous sound studio, and the scene called for an outrageous musical extravaganza. Willis had lights hanging all over the place; the ceiling was thick with barndoors. He stood there, looking over his set, appraising the lighting. Calling over one of his assistants, Willis pointed to one of the hundreds of lights on the ceiling. "That bulb is weak," he said. When the bulb was replaced and the old one was tested, it was weaker by fifty watts or so. Willis was able to discern that by simply looking at the set. That is the sign of a well-trained eye that you can count on to light anything. It's the kind of skill that everyone wants to have working on his video production.

You may have guessed by now that the gaffer and the cameraman have an important relationship: One is completely dependent on the other. Many productions employ what is called a lighting cameraman who can do both jobs. But remember that the lighting cameraman is doing the thinking of two people, and he is well aware of the complexities involved in either job separately.

When a production is in the preproduction stage and the crew has been hired, the gaffer gets together with the cameraman to discuss the look of the project. Of course, their decisions depend on the wishes of the director, but a director with a good gaffer and cameraman trusts their judgment and allows them to do their best work, as long as it follows his dictate.

Once the "look" has been agreed upon, the gaffer and the cameraman set out to achieve that goal. Since the cameraman enjoys a little more power than does the gaffer, the gaffer does everything to suit his wishes as well. Many cameramen have their own preferences, no matter what the project entails. That might mean that he wants a lot of depth in every shot, which means a lot of light. Another cameraman may like a lot of camera movement, which means the gaffer has to light a large area so that the camera movement is not restricted. It is important that the cameraman make his requirements clear to the gaffer, so that there is a minimum of disagreement on the set. If the gaffer and the cameraman have essential stylistic differences—say the cameraman loves the gritty, realist look whereas the gaffer likes a softer look—they will never get along on the set. It is up to the director to exercise his control, iron out any differences, and negotiate a truce between the two. But the chances are that it will be an uneasy truce, with a lot of grumbling among the crew.

Hostility on the set between essential crew members is instant death for a production. It wastes time and money, it sometimes ruins reputations, the project drags on and on, and everybody wishes it were over. That does not make for the most creative environment for any kind of program. Often such disagreements arise out of ignorance. If you know your craft, understanding its function both as an entity and as a contribution to a production, your peers are more likely to respect your opinions. The only quality of a gaffer that is better than expertise is the ability to cooperate and assist what has to be a team effort.

Camera Operator
There is more to a camera than operation. It represents the eye of every viewer who will ever see your work. It

is the point of view from which we gain information about what we see. Camera placement, movement, and focus can all make their own statements about the subject. When Alfred Hitchcock wanted a character to look weak and helpless, he shot him from high above, which gave the viewer a feeling of power. Since then, that camera angle has served as a code for a helpless character. Close-ups are intimate, revealing, compelling. Charlie Chaplin said that his rule was a close-up for drama, a wide shot for comedy. The rule still stands. The craft of a cameraman is loaded with rules like that, and inventive cameramen have been breaking them for years. But you can't break a rule unless you know it, have used it, and understand its meaning. That takes practice and cunning and a little something extra that we call "a good eye."

The simple act of placing a square border around any subject opens up a can of worms. Let's say the subject is a face. Just a face. What can you do with that? The first problem that comes to mind is lighting. What kind of face are we looking at: mean, friendly, gorgeous, hideous, meaningless? A bare bulb hanging over the subject's head will make him look stark and desperate. Lighting from underneath will make him look like Dracula. A little diffusion from the side and some backlight on the hair will give him a halo worthy of an angel. Only backlight will make him look sinister and mysterious, or just lonely. Fully frontal lighting will produce a flat, documentary, honest look.

Once you have exhausted all of the possibilities of lighting, and chosen one, it's time to choose the camera angle accordingly.

In one shot alone, such as a character answering the phone, slamming the receiver down, grabbing his coat and bolting out of the door, you may have three or four angles at work simultaneously, as well as three lens posi-

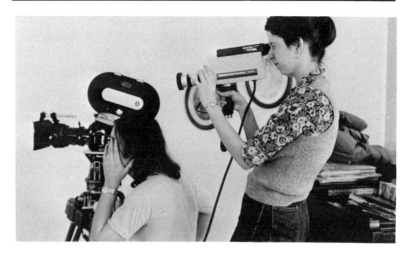

The video camera is a cheap and effective way to do camera rehearsals without wasting expensive film.

tions. Lighting, focal length, and camera angle work together in a complex yet fluid way that gives us not only the basic information about the subject, but also the way we react to that subject.

When you start adding more than one subject to the frame, especially another character, the variables increase dramatically, as does our perception of what is happening right before our eyes. The camera is our eyes, and we rely on it to show us what we need to see and what we want to know.

I won't go into all of the technical and stylistic choices that a cameraman has to make, because that information has filled a mountain of excellent books on the subject. But it is important that you be aware of demands and responsibilities of the camera operator.

The cameraman and the director have the closest working relationship on a video production. The director depends upon his cameraman to give him what he wants on the screen. Because of this, they go through a

Action!

long period of discussion deciding what to do on the set, and sometimes they shoot test footage to see if they are getting the look that best suits the production. If the video footage looks bad, it is the cameraman's fault. If the footage looks fantastic, the director is a genius. Directors are well aware of this relationship, and any director who looks like a genius will want to look like a genius again. He will work with the same cameraman who served so well before. Woody Allen has used Gordon Willis as his cinematographer for years, and the result has been a consistent look in his films that can be identified immediately as a Woody Allen production. The point is that the cameraman has to deal with a great deal of pressure and responsibility, and he uses some very specific tools toward that end.

Technical expertise is the most important requirement. That is true of any craft, but with a cameraman it must be a given. It means a thorough knowledge of the properties of light, lenses, tape stock, movement, and every camera on the market. To utilize this knowledge he must have keen eyes and the steady hands of a demolition expert. The cameraman must be so proficient in these areas that his work is flawlessly consistent.

The demands on a cameraman are great because the viewer has become so sophisticated. Thanks to uncountable hours spent in front of the television set, your basic ten-year-old has developed an acute sense of how a television picture should look. The familiar set-up of a TV newscaster looking into the camera is one that we take for granted. But if the newscaster is a little off-center or the slightest bit out of focus, we see it immediately and recognize it as a mistake. There are basic skills that a cameraman must develop in order to be successful and satisfy the viewer, and they are not as simple as you might think.

The most basic skill that a cameraman must learn is to frame the subject in an acceptable composition and keep him in focus. Once you have this elemental training, you're ready for the big, bad world of video production.

The studio is a good place to learn how to use a video camera. Chances are that you'll be operating a decent camera on a good tripod with wheels, and there is someone in the control booth who will tell you what to do. The controlled environment of the studio is perfect for learning the basics of camerawork within a relatively rigid structure. Since there are usually two or three cameras on the floor, you will be working in conjunction with other camera operators at the same time on the same show, and the total responsibility for the picture won't rest on your shoulders alone.

When you are shooting on location, it is desirable to duplicate the controlled environment of the studio. That

The studio cameraman gets his marching orders through the headsets.

eliminates the potential for hang-ups that can kill a production. But, like the gaffer who must improvise on a location set, the cameraman has many more variables to deal with when he is in the field.

The cameraman's first step outside of the studio is usually an ENG production. ENG is really just a technical title for a small crew shooting news bits to be used as part of a news broadcast. The ENG crew consists of the cameraman, a soundman, and a reporter. Sometimes the cameraman attaches a microphone to the camera or simply hands the mic to the reporter, thereby eliminating the soundman from the crew. This sort of crew is called a "one-man band." The one-man band does everything but stand in front of his own camera, and it's a sure sign of a low-budget production. I can't guarantee that you won't lose your mind working as a one-man band, but with all of that equipment strapped to your back and on your shoulders, there is a good chance that you'll begin to feel like a turtle.

Let's assume that your producer provides your ENG crew with a soundman and all you have to worry about is the camera. What kinds of situations can you expect to encounter as an ENG cameraman?

One thing you can expect is that you will not always have the benefit of a tripod. ENG crews work fast and furious (*i.e.*, "down and dirty") and seldom shoot more than fifty seconds of tape at one time. Because of the brevity that our cursory news coverage demands, the ENG crew strives to minimize the set-up time for every shot. Often the ENG crew has several stories to cover in a day, and so they spend as little time as possible at each location. What does that mean? A lot of hand-held camera shooting. The ENG cameraman is always shooting from the hip, always keeping one eye out for action while the other is glued to the eyepiece. That is why your typical local news location footage is far from spectacular. This is news: All of the rules of documentaries apply. Rough camerawork, poor lighting, soft focus, everything goes. As an ENG cameraman, you get only one shot at a story, and whatever you get goes on the air that very evening.

A magazine format show uses an ENG crew, but because it falls under the heading of entertainment and information, the news and documentary rules no longer apply, nor does the demand for brevity. The simple reason is that shows like "60 Minutes" and "Entertainment Tonight" can take a little more time to develop a story, so the crew can take a little more time shooting it. The type of shooting you might do for a show of this kind would be interview set-ups, documenting a process such as hairdressing or shoemaking, and shooting a performance. What it all adds up to is that shooting for the magazine show requires ENG

NAME YOUR POISON

skills with a dash of care and the luxury of a lighter schedule.

Shooting a commercial means that you will be working from a shooting script of some kind, and you'll have a much larger crew to help you. The requirements of a commercial are very strict, because the requirements of the station broadcasting the commercial are very strict. If a commercial has to come in at twenty-nine and a half seconds exactly, then every shot in the commercial will be timed out to fit within that time. That means you have to make the shot work according to the restrictions that you are given. If a move is complicated, it is possible to do several takes before you get it right. The first might be too slow; the second, too fast. Shooting a commercial is a very trying experience because of all of the demands, but a good-looking commercial on your reel is helpful when you're looking for work.

Many of the same rules for the commercial shoot apply to shooting industrials, promotionals, and narratives. But as you move into these more demanding jobs, you'll need a few more skills at your disposal. Directors like working with a cameraman who knows how to light a set and do it quickly. Sometimes you'll have a gaffer to work with on this, and sometimes you won't. Either way, efficiency is just as important as experience. Shooting an industrial, a promotional, or a narrative means working on a major scale with a lot of talented technicians. It means that your work will be under intense scrutiny. It means knowing what to do, taking your time doing it, and doing it right.

Perhaps the greatest challenge to a video cameraman is the shooting of a documentary, because it demands the alertness of the ENG cameraman and the manipulative skills of the narrative shooter. The ENG cameraman gets what he has to get and exits. The documentary cameraman gets what he has to get and makes it look good.

There is something about a documentary cameraman that cannot be taught: the ability to see everything that is happening around him, locate whatever is most important, and shoot it effectively, constantly repeating the process as he shoots. It has something to do with anticipation and peripheral vision. That "something" is a valuable asset to any cameraman.

The camera operator should be able to shoot news, ENG, magazine format, industrial, promotional, narrative, commercial, and documentary. One leads to another; one feeds off of another. In fact, if you choose a career as a cameraman, you can't help but learn all of these things, regardless of the field in which you make your start.

Engineer

Engineers are a breed apart. They are isolated from video production, yet they are absolutely essential. Engineers are the inventors and the repairmen. They have the X-ray vision of a mechanic. Video would be nowhere without them.

Video decks and cameras, not to mention all of the additional equipment, are intensely complicated machines. A video deck is stuffed with circuit boards and crammed with wires and diodes, all of which can malfunction after the slightest jolt. Cameras are worse because they are light-sensitive and convert light into electric pulses. That's why we have so many automatic cameras—to keep our undereducated fingers away from things that we don't understand. The problem is, the more automatic features that are built into a camera, the more complex it becomes. Call in the engineers!

The great thing about engineers is that they understand every piece of equipment, right down to the last

Name Your Poison

fuse. But without exception, the engineer's first question will be, "Is it plugged in?" Often it is not plugged in. Even if it is, that relatively simple question brings you down to earth when you are suffering from an acute case of technical anxiety. "Is it really broken, or am I just forgetting something?" Only the engineer knows for sure.

I have been in that situation a few times, especially when working with computers for editing. We had a one-inch VTR that wouldn't do what we told it to. After a series of tests, I had no satisfactory results. Call the engineer. The engineer arrived, and we all stood expectantly around the one-inch machine. The engineer opened the machine. We gasped. A forty-thousand-dollar machine! The engineer was rooting through the wires, poking and muttering. He pulled out a circuit board and blew on it. He put it back. Then he carefully pulled out his screwdriver, grabbed it by the metal bit, and began whacking the insides of the VTR. Smack, smack, crack! He slammed the machine shut and turned it on and off a few times. Then he thumped it a good one, right on top. We tried it. It worked.

Now the engineer no longer asks me if the machine is plugged in. He says, "Did you try turning it on and off?" I say yes. I know what's coming next. "Did you beat on it a little?"

Besides these voodoo practices of the engineer, there are some very concrete advantages to having one around to look after your equipment. First of all, only an engineer can do it right. If someone pretends to be an engineer and starts poking and whacking, he might poke in the wrong place and you're out forty thousand dollars. But the greatest advantage to having an engineer around is that he can identify problems quickly and repair them equally fast. That means money in the bank for the equipment owner. Why? Because for every minute that a piece of equipment is broken, or "down," you can't make money with it, which is why you bought it in the first place. "Downtime" can become very expensive if you don't repair the faulty equipment right away.

Of all the technicians who are involved with video production on any level, the engineer is the only one who gets his training in school. A lot of math and science is involved, as well as practice, practice, practice. None of the training grounds that I have outlined will suffice. Going to engineering school is a necessary investment and a secure commitment to your trade.

POSTPRODUCTION
Editor

When the shooting schedule has been completed and everyone is happy with the footage, the tapes are brought to the editor. The video tape editor pieces together the footage into a completed program.

There is a tenuous relationship between the camera operator and the editor. Because of that, cameramen make good editors and editors make excellent cameramen. If the cameraman has a good sense of how to put a program together in postproduction, he will be careful to provide the editor with crucial close-ups and cuttable angles; he'll give every shot plenty of lead time and plenty at the end, so the editor will have enough material to work with; and he'll see to it that his best shots are put together properly so that they make it into the program.

An important fact to remember is that when a production is completed in the field and taken into postproduction, nearly everyone who worked on the production is gone, working on other projects, and the editor is left to work with material that is basically unal-

NAME YOUR POISON

Now we're talking! This is an on-line computer editing system.

terable. The editor has to work with the material that he is given. Sometimes the work the editor does on questionable material has amazing results.

Most video editing is done with two machines: a playback deck and a record deck. The editor selects scenes from the player and builds an edited master on the recorder. This is called "off-line" editing because the "line" refers to a gamut of effects that can be implemented between the player and the recorder.

Off-line editing systems are now primarily the computer's territory. By recording video tape onto a hard drive—a process called "digitizing"—the material, though compressed, can now be accessed in what is called a "non-linear" fashion. This means the editor can grab a shot from any part of a show, and move it to another section in an instant, much as you would "drag and drop" a computer file from one folder to another. This process makes editing much faster, although it requires a lot of horsepower in the computer. Typical non-linear editing systems are Avid (at the high end) and Adobe Premiere (at the low end). Needless to say, as computers evolve, and compression improves, these two "ends" will move closer together.

Once the sequence is edited on the computer, the editor can output the show directly from the computer onto tape. At present, this procedure is considered "non-broadcast," since video compression does not meet certain quality standards as of yet. Another method of finishing a show is to output an edit list, which is a list of numbers that record each shot, and the order of the shots. The list can be taken to an on-line room, and the show reconstituted in a broadcast form.

The "on-line" editing facility requires much more skill with video machines. The simplest on-line set-up would be the addition of a TBC processing amplifier to the video feed coming out of the player. A TBC strips the video image into four primary elements (video level, black level, chroma level, and hue level), so that you can control each element separately.

You would use a TBC if a tape came in underexposed or filtered incorrectly, and the TBC would permit you to change the colors of a subject on the tape. Another neat trick of the TBC is to stabilize a picture that's jumping around or jittering for some technical reason. It provides a new, strong sync pulse that matches the one on the tape and stabilizes almost anything. The purpose of this is to allow you to dissolve between *two* playback decks onto one record deck without the considerable problems that might ensue. By adding a video switcher into the system, the on-line editor can dissolve, wipe, fade—whatever the switcher is capable of doing to a video image.

It is evident that an editor working with an on-line system has many more options than the off-line editor, but on-line editing also requires more technical expertise. Because the on-line editor may have to alter video images, utilize a switcher, and even run a computer, he needs to have the knowledge of an engineer. When a system becomes that complicated, the number of things that can go wrong is staggering. And many on-line systems are built with equipment from many different companies. For example, you might have Sony decks, a Grass Valley switcher, a CMX 340 computer keyboard, an Ampex I-square system, and a Teac audio board. Sometimes those guys don't get along. The editor has to be a technical diplomat who can negotiate between the machines and get everything to work together.

It that were all it took to be an editor, you might say that an engineer would make an excellent editor. Not true. The technical expertise is only the requirement for employment and the foundation on which you build your experience. Once you have the fundamentals down, it's time to get into the real work of the editor.

The "real work" of the editor is to take materials from different sources and make them look as if they were meant to be together. That takes some skill in pacing, directing, and even writing. If you think of a half-hour soap opera as thirty minutes of script, then it is up to the editor to see that the script makes sense. Sometimes it doesn't make sense on paper and it doesn't make sense in the order in which it was shot. The editor restructures the material so that it *works*.

Once the program has been shot, the editor absorbs

the jobs of many people on the set. He becomes the writer, the director, and the architect. And this is true of any kind of video production, whether it is a glossy docudrama or a commercial for a used-car lot.

One of the toughest aspects of being a video editor has nothing to do with technical expertise or creativity. Staff and freelance editors frequently work with many clients every day. You could be the greatest editor in the world, but if you can't get along with a director or an advertising executive, you'll never work. Most clients want some creative input when they're working, they want assistance in making decisions, they want your advice. If the advice is good and the show works, that client will come back time and time again because he is happy and he trusts your judgment. That is how you build a clientele.

Like the cameraman who can work with many different situations, the editor should be flexible. The video editor ought to be able to push buttons; that much is obvious. And when it is required, the editor ought to be able to offer creative advice. It is important to develop a rapport with the client that is mutually creative. After all, the material that goes onto the master edit tape is the final product, the reconstitution of the broken egg. If the client strides out of the door happy with work he's done, then you will work again.

Sound Mixer

This job is not much different from that of the production audio engineer, except that the postproduction sound mixer is working with prerecorded material. It is more likely that the audio engineer will work in both production and preproduction.

In most cases, the video editor is also expected to serve as a sound mixer. Few editing rooms have more than one person working in these areas. Fewer video

Name Your Poison

The postproduction audio mixing board. Next to it is the keyboard of the Chyron character generator.

editors have exceptional skills at sound mixing. An editor who can handle both professionally is valuable to an editing facility that employs only video editors and character generator operators.

Character Generator Operator

The character generator (CG) operator types up the letters, or characters, that appear on the television screen. The most common use of the CG is the "lower thirds super," which translates into a name superimposed on the lower third of the screen. You see this a lot on news interviews, when a subject is talking and his or her name pops onto the screen under the chin. It is simply a way to tell the audience who is doing the talking.

Other uses of the CG include titles, disclaimers, information such as graphs, and of course, commercials.

The television commercial gets the most out of the CG because it has so much information to impart in so short a time. The character generator is a cheap way to get your message across, since it doesn't require a camera or a face or lights or any of the common production requirements. Just put the name of the product up there, get someone to read the copy, and you've got your spot. Low-budget commercials are full of CG material, and they bombard you during the Late Late Show.

The CG operator works in the postproduction editing facility, providing the client with whatever is needed on the screen. Some new character generators can provide volumes of pages, each with different type styles, or fonts, a rainbow of colors, a variety of edge types, outlines, shadow borders, crawls, spot shadows, just about anything you can come up with for your particular message. The CG operator conjures all of the effects that the client wants by pecking away at a keyboard and storing the information in a small computer.

Because the CG operation is time-consuming, the video editor is relieved of the duty in order to save the client time and money. The CG operator gets the information from the client in advance and stores the effects before the edit session gets under way. That way, when the edit session is in full gear, the CG operator can simply call up the desired characters and the editor can punch them right in.

The CG operator does not have a very glamorous job, but if you watch enough television, you know that video productions get a lot of mileage out of the character generator. It is a good skill to add to your list of marketable skills.

Special Effects Generator Operator

That is a pretty long title for a specific job: operating the special effects generator (SEG) in video postpro-

Name Your Poison

duction. As special effects become more spectacular and more complicated, computers become the standard tool of the SEG operator. That doesn't mean that you have to go to computer school. Just be aware that the machines that provide these effects are crammed with testy little computer chips that are very complicated. The only way to learn to run one is to work with the exact machine that you plan to use. That means hanging around a postproduction facility that can afford these outrageously expensive toys and getting someone to show you how to run one.

Because the SEG is expensive to buy, and even to rent, the operator makes a good wage in exchange for knowledge and the ability to work quickly. Some of these effects—such as the *ADO*, which flips an image every which way without any breakup—can cost a client as much as $800 an hour to use. The client can get very nervous when he's laying out that kind of money, and he wants the job done right, efficiently. As more and more upscale productions utilize the SEG, the demand grows for operators who are proficient in this field.

Many affordable computer software programs emulate the special effects generators used in these facilities. The facilities do not use these programs as of yet, because they are slow and less flexible than the really expensive boxes. But for learning purposes, these software programs are an excellent tool. Many of the lower-budget productions are using off-the-shelf software to produce trailblazing effects, and the heavy-hitting producers are following their lead. Now that you can learn to use this type of software at home or at school, you can get a head start on your career as a special effects expert, and be sure that your services will only be in greater demand as time goes by.

The demand for proficient technicians and nontechnicians grows daily as the video production business booms. The aspiring novice has to make a lot of decisions as to which jobs will suit you and your needs. As you can see, there are many, many jobs to choose from, and the training for each one differs slightly as to where to get it and how long it will take. When it comes time to step into the fray, you'll have to ask yourself some questions, and the answers will design an agenda for your career.

5

Having What It Takes

Choosing a career doesn't necessarily mean a lot of soul-searching. Your future is not a void that is waiting to be filled by strokes of luck and fortune or molded by fate. There are actually some guidelines that you have set out for yourself without even knowing it. Your behavior, your ambition, your simple likes and dislikes, your favorite food, favorite movies and books, and your current taste for adventure or stability will all combine to direct you in your choice.

When you think about a career in video, start at the top and work your way down through the so-called "requirements" of the business. Remember that though none of them is etched in stone, some of the requirements can give you an idea of which career best suits your personality.

What is your goal? Do you want to be the whiz-kid video producer who turns the business upside down? You can direct if you like. Or you can be the best cameraman ever to look through a lens. Writing might be for you, or maybe you'd like to run a video studio as a floor manager. You know what jobs are available to you, and some of them look better than others. Find the one that represents your career goal, and then find the best way to achieve it.

The best way to achieve your goal is to get the best possible training. University training is good for some careers and bad for others. An internship might better suit your choice. Look over Chapter 3, "The Training Ground," and see where you might get the best experience for your particular choice.

Sometimes that choice will consist of the decision to enter the video production business, period. You may not know exactly what you want to do *within* the field, just as the student who enters medical school doesn't know whether she wants to specialize in pediatrics or nose surgery. There is a period during which your attitude will decide your future in video.

What kind of attitude does video production require? One of the greatest assets you can have is resourcefulness. You will not always have the best equipment or personnel or a lot of money to work with. But it is not enough to "make do." In any stage of a video production, every decision that you make depends upon your resources. And the success of the production, as well as your job, depends upon your ability to squeeze the last drop out of those resources.

Part of being successful is the ability to troubleshoot. No matter what your task, you will be confronted with failures and breakdowns of all kinds. They could be equipment failures or the failure of an actor to show up on time on the set. Problems of that kind require immediate attention. If you have a tendency to throw your hands up and walk away from problems, the business of video may not be for you. But if you look catastrophe in the eye, wrestle it down, and fix problems as good as new, you'll go a long way.

Troubleshooting often takes a good deal of improvisation. If you are in the field shooting and someone forgot to bring the boom, a screaming match with the soundman will get everybody nowhere. But by commandeering a broomstick and some gaffer's tape, you've got the production moving again. Even a well-organized production relies on a certain amount of improvisation to cope with the unpredictable problems that are bound to occur.

Resourcefulness, troubleshooting, and improvisation take a certain amount of imagination. These attributes are all interrelated, and they can erase the frustrations that frequently accompany video production. Imagination and related abilities can help you make those decisions and solve problems.

As handy as it may sound, imagination is clearly not enough to see you through a career in video. The bottom line is that you *must know your tools*. It's impossible to improvise under the gun when you haven't the faintest idea what you're working with. You can't be resourceful if you aren't familiar with your resources. And you can't shoot troubles if your gun isn't loaded. It may sound trite, but ask any shoemaker or blacksmith or bulldozer driver, and they'll tell you. Know your tools. Know everybody else's tools. It'll pay off in the pinch.

There is another attitude that can be helpful to you in the video business, or any other business, for that matter: determination. Video is very competitive, and the people who make it in the business are determined to do so. That goes especially for job-seeking, which is the all-time super-frustration in any business. If you convince yourself that you *have* to get that job, you'll get it, because the employer senses your determination and wants that attitude to work for him.

While determination may help you fix your purpose, aggressiveness will help you achieve it. That doesn't mean that you must have an aggressive nature, or that you need to storm production houses in order to get a job. But a little aggressiveness at the right time can do wonders.

When it comes to using them, neither of these attributes is limited to seeking jobs. Once you are on the job, you should be determined to complete it successfully. If your job is hampered by someone's interference, you should be aggressive enough to surmount it without hindering your position. Your primary goal is to succeed in your task. For every aggressive move you make, you'll use a touch of diplomacy to offset the effects.

It is important to maintain a balance among all of the communicative skills at your disposal when working in video. A character who is always aggressive will alienate himself from his peers and especially from work. An overly passive character will be easily forgotten when hiring time comes around. This "balance" boils down to consistency, which applies to attitude and work habits.

Aside from personal characteristics, I think consistency plays a bigger role when it comes down to the actual work that you do. Of course, the ideal is to be consistently perfect, but ho! Never heard of it. Can't be done. It pays to be dependable, which is what consistency is all about. Your client or your boss or your friends have certain expectations of you, based on past relationships. A good cameraman is someone you can depend on to deliver a good picture consistently, from job to job, and, surprise!, that takes a whole other set of attitudes.

It helps to be patient in the video business. Sometimes it helps to be patient *with* the video business, which means putting up with the inconsistencies and catastrophes that come naturally to video. Beyond that, there are singular situations that require a good deal of patience. The most obvious situation is job-seeking. For every aggressive move that you make, for every sizzling interview, you'll need the patience that it takes to wait for that important phone call and to accept it if someone else gets the job. This is especially true for the freelancer, who lives from job to job without any real security besides talent. There are so many jobs to be had, and so much work to be done, that you'll just have to buck up and rebound from the inevitable disappointments.

While you are employed on a production, there will be situations particular to that job that require patience: equipment malfunctions, operator malfunctions, mistakes, and other setbacks. For instance, if you've set up for an exterior shot that requires bright sunlight, and the clouds move in, you'll have to wait patiently for the sun to break through and be ready to make your shot when it does. That means you have to hang loose while the clock ticks away and the sun hangs laughing behind a cloud.

The fact that you have to contend with nuisances and be prepared to act when they are resolved means that you must always be alert on the job. When the sun breaks and it's time to move, it helps to know when to move and how. That can get hairy when people are scurrying about asking questions and money is being spent and you've put expensive people on hold. But knowing how to move confidently when the crisis hits is the key to keeping the production from certain collapse.

The client puts bread in your pocket, but he can also be a perfect nuisance during a production. You cannot fire a client. The client is the customer, and you know what they say about customers' right to be right at any cost. At times a difficult client can give you a colossal headache over details, but if you don't take care of him with a smile on your face, the customer takes his budget elsewhere.

When it comes to clients, it helps to have what is called a good bedside manner. The same goes for working with other people in your field. Again, that goes back to the bit about balancing your aggression with quiet determination. Your rapport with the people you work with, whether in or outside of a production, is the real nuts and bolts of your career. Since so many video jobs stem from previous productions and word-of-mouth references, your behavior will be remembered every bit as much as your proficiency. The know-it-all who bristles at the slightest criticism will not have a long career in video. Video production is a collaborative business, made up of a wide variety of people who handle specific crucial stages of the production, and everyone relies on one another to make the show a success.

What kinds of people are in the video field? It's easy to say that all kinds are there, but there are some specific types that pop up on every production.

One type is the determined professional. He is the one who is determined to succeed at any cost, and not necessarily in an egotistical way. The production is his one and only concern, and his devotion to that project is all-consuming. If you can do your job well, you will work extremely well with this type. If you are error-prone, however, he will see to it that you're not on the set the next day.

Anyone who is in the video business strives to become a determined professional. Some make it and some don't. It takes a lot of conviction and strength, and it should be obvious that the more determined professionals you have on a production, the better it will look.

There are some people who behave like determined professionals but are actually quite unprofessional and determined only to further their own career and boost their ego. Most of this type are on-camera personalities who thrive on exposure of any kind, as long as it is their good side. They will drive you crazy. The unfortunate thing is that the obnoxious extrovert as an on-camera talent wields lots of power because it is his or her face that everybody sees, and you may well be responsible for how it looks on the television screen. The extrovert will stick to you like glue to make sure you don't damage his appearance or make him look bad. Patience comes in handy here, as well as a pair of ear plugs.

Another type you might run into is the perfectionist. The perfectionist is a little like a determined professional but is obsessed with detail. I would rather have a perfectionist on my crew than an irresponsible person, but there are times when a perfectionist can slow down a production with endless tweakings and adjustments that could be meaningless in the long run. A perfectionist client is another story, because they are so difficult. Some clients are pussycats, others are bears; but a perfectionist will test all of your patience and most of your bedside manner. But why worry about that? You should be able to turn in a "perfect" product, perfected along the guidelines of the client, if necessary. It's just not as much fun.

You can lump a lot of the remaining types under the heading of "hacks." A hack is someone who has been doing the same thing for years with little noticeable improvement in performance. A hack will get work and provide an acceptable product, but don't expect grand results. All that is really missing is the fierce ambition of the determined pro.

I grant that the description of four types is hardly comprehensive, but it will give you an idea of what types to look out for and what to become or avoid. What one really wants to become is successful, and there are some types of people who consistently succeed in the video business.

A self-starter is someone who will have a successful career in video. He's eager and innovative with a lot of gas in his tank. I suppose that most people in the business are self-starters of some kind, or they never would have gotten into the field to begin with. But once you get your first break, it is important not to lose the drive that put you there.

Originators and innovators will always have a place in video. I think that is true for any business, and the rule holds in video. Producers latch onto creativity wherever they spot it, because it is extremely valuable to have creative people around when you're working in a creative medium. It is not something easily taught, but if you have it, rest assured that you won't go hungry during your career in video.

The remainder of the successful types can be divided into two categories: the settlers and the climbers. The settler finds his niche and devotes all of his energy to a specific job. VTR operators, cameramen, production managers, and sound engineers are good examples of this type. The settler soon becomes an expert in his field and a valuable commodity. I like to work with these people because they have come to a decision about their careers and have stuck with it. That is the sure sign of the determined professional.

The climber is an ambitious sort with an eye on the Big Top. Every job is a step toward the next one, and every level is meant to be departed for the next. Climbing is both tricky and natural. It seems natural to move up during a career, but doing so can be a problem if it isn't addressed properly. The climber needs to have that good rapport, as well as a thorough understanding of everybody's job. It takes a lot of time and patience, and if the climber hits a snag, his lack of expertise may hurt him if he has to fall back on a previous position that he doesn't know terribly well.

It's nearly impossible to *choose* any one type for yourself when weighing your prospective career in video. It is more likely that you *are* a type, or leaning toward a certain attitude toward your work, and that will determine your eventual position within the video industry.

It will take a bit of self-evaluation and a little study to figure out where your career in video might go. If you could chart your preference of jobs, your attitude, and your personal qualities, you might be able to predict how and where your career in video would lead you.

6

The Rewards

Whatever career you choose, you want to feel satisfied and happy with your choice. In choosing a career in video, you will find many kinds of rewards.

FINANCIAL

The video industry can provide some financial rewards that are very enticing. Nearly every position pays well except for the hapless production assistant. Once you have paid your dues and shown yourself capable, the pay is good. Unfortunately, most people in video pay their dues as production assistants.

How much do video positions pay? That depends on a few variables: location, experience, and professional position. By "professional position" I mean choosing between two positions that pay differently: the staff position and the freelancer.

A staff position pays less than freelance wages because the work is guaranteed over the workweek. That means security for the staff employee, security at a good wage, and that is hard to pass up. As a staff camera operator, for example, you can expect to make at least $200 a day, depending upon whether you are in the union or not. Union pay is higher, but union dues are worse than taxes. Staff employees can expect some medical

The Rewards

benefits, regular pay raises, and planned vacations. A staff position permits you to plan your life and your career to a certain extent, which is mighty handy in the unstable world of television.

The freelancer really walks the edge between living high on the hog and taking long, unpaid, unscheduled vacations. The daily rate of a freelancer is higher than that of a staff employee, which makes up for the periodic stretches when the freelancer has no work. The benefits are a good measure of professional freedom: freedom to choose the jobs you want to do, go where you want to go. Some freelancers work as much as staff employees because they have a solid list of regular clients, but that is uncommon. For the most part, freelancing is an unstable, uncertain way to go, but for my money it's more exciting. A freelance cameraman can pull in $350 a day for a few days' work. But if you average that high pay with the days when there is no work, the money evens out. So what it boils down to is temperament. Some people want the security of a full-time job; others are pleased with the freedom that freelancing offers. Put it on your chart and see where you fit into the scheme.

Personal Satisfaction

That is where the real "money" is: happiness. A career in video can give you many moments of satisfaction within a short time. One major creative achievement per year is more than many people in other jobs ever see, and in the video business you may have several. You get a real feeling of accomplishment, no matter what your job entails, when you see a production of yours on television. It's a way to reach people. And it's a way to find yourself—to reveal how well you work and relate with people.

Travel Opportunities

A career in video offers many possibilities for travel whether you work on a staff or as a freelancer. Virtually every nonstudio production goes on location, so you get to spend some time out of the office and in the street. Not every job allows for this, but you have to remember that we're talking about the minimum amount of travel. Many productions take place out of town, sometimes in exotic locations. As a cameraman, I had the opportunity to travel to Bulgaria and shoot for two weeks in a country that I might otherwise never have seen. Forays into the countryside are not uncommon, nor are shoots that require a few weeks away from home. On the larger productions, the producer would probably take many more personnel along to keep things running smoothly.

Think of video production as an ongoing search for material that is available anytime and anywhere, and, as a member of the video industry, it is up to you to find it. If you like to travel, video is a career that offers a lot of it. You don't have to do it if you don't want to. That includes even the minor travel. I know someone who refuses to shoot anything from a helicopter. For her, helicopters are doomsday machines and there is no way she'll ever climb into one, even if it means losing that particular job. She won't lose all of her work because of her fear of helicopters (heliaphobia?), and she doesn't lack for other work. Someone else who loves shooting from helicopters will do it. Likewise, you might be asked to scale mountains, lower yourself into a copper mine, hang from fire escapes, and stand close to the whirl of natural disasters. For every thriller you get, there will be lost-cat stories and sewer system scandals to even out the excitement. But the excitement is there! You want it, you got it!

THE REWARDS

The Public Forum

Reaching the public forum is a little like the creative satisfaction of a career in video, with a bit of self-righteousness thrown in for good measure. Television reaches more people than do newspapers or movies. That is the public forum. In the video industry, you can reach all of those people with your message. That message can be political, artistic, or documentary. The possibilities are endless. As a producer, you can put together a program that exposes injustice or illuminates your ideals. If it is done properly, your program will reach many people and elicit an immediate response when other media will not. If you have an immediate story or message, no other means will reach so many people so fast. Of course, most people who watch commercial television aren't interested in messages, but maybe that is exactly what you want to change. Good luck.

7

Being Your Own Boss

In Chapter 1, I described how much video business was available and how it was growing in quantum leaps. That hasn't changed by this chapter. There is plenty of business out there, ripe for the picking. And the great thing about video is that you can become your own boss at a relatively early stage and enjoy some success. You may want to open your own production house and shoot for other people on a lens-for-hire basis. That "hired gun" approach is the most popular among young video entrepreneurs. The same goes for postproduction facilities; you might set up a shop where people can come with their unedited work and have you chop it for them. Most of the self-employed video industrialists are involved in the technical end, that is, production or postproduction, and all it really takes to do so is an investment. But how and where do you make that big move?

The first step is to find a good location with a hearty appetite for your business. Los Angeles probably has a bigger appetite than Barnesville, Ohio. That is no secret, and as a result, the competition in a place like Los Angeles is very stiff, precisely because there is so much business to be had. So you'll have to measure your own appetite for competition against your potential location. It may be that Barnesville doesn't have a video production facility and needs one, so that your arrival will immediately pick up all the work that is available. You can run a very satisfying business and develop a decent demo reel that you can take to a larger market when the time calls for it. Or you can go to the major markets (New York, Los Angeles, Chicago, Houston) and try your hand there. It may be tough at first, but once you get a foothold in a large market, your business can escalate quickly.

If you are going to start your own business in production or postproduction, you'll need equipment. You can go two ways with this: Buy it or rent it. Among theories about solving this dilemma, one says that buying is best. For an initial investment of thirty grand or so, you can own a respectable production package that includes a good video camera, a 3/4-inch deck, a light kit, and an all-purpose sound rig. Since you won't have to rent anything, all that you make can go back into the business, and you can recoup your investment within one productive year or so. From then on your only expense is maintenance. A thirty-thousand-dollar investment is nothing for a bank to issue, and if you have a decent credit rating you can be on your way in no time.

Purchasing equipment has some very real drawbacks, however. The most serious one is that so-called state-of-the-art equipment can become obsolete fast. Video engineering is still in its formative stages, the industry is in flux, and a camera that you thought was the last word in electronic photography may look more and more ancient as cameras enter the market that are twice as good and half as expensive. On top of that rather risky proposition, the cost of video maintenance can kill you if your equipment breaks down a lot. Unless you can handle day-to-day repairs and maintenance, I don't recommend this route, especially for a beginner.

I like the rental route because you won't have to fool with overhead such as maintenance, replacement parts, and exorbitant insurance. Let someone else worry about that, and rent your equipment from him. By renting, you have the flexibility to choose the equipment that best suits the needs of the job: state-of-the-art camera or a high-end industrial camera, 1-inch, 3/4-inch, or 1/2-inch, lots of light or no light at all. You can put together your own package by renting from one group or from several. And when the shoot is finished, you can return the equipment and not think about it until the next job. Meanwhile, the renter is tweaking and monitoring the equipment so it is in good shape for the next rental.

One of the drawbacks of renting video equipment is that, since video engineering is stuck with equipment that many other producers or technicians have had their hands on, you may suddenly discover that your deck is acting strangely because the last renter spilled a milkshake into it.

The other drawback to rental is the killer: money. It costs more to rent. The reason is obvious: If somebody invests in a video rig when he buys it, he's going to try to make some of it back when he rents it to you. As a result, he has to charge you the rental fee plus a fee for himself. Equipment owners don't have to do that since they don't have to rent, and their rates tend to be lower than those of a producer who rents. The renter becomes a middleman of sorts, renting from one business and then renting the same thing to his client. Since most rentals require a deposit, renting can put a crimp in your cash flow. But if you can handle all that, the freedom and convenience of renting outweigh the hassle of ownership.

One of the big differences between owning and renting is its effect on your mobility. Buying a lot of expensive equipment means a heavy commitment to the location you've chosen as your market. It is not easy to pack up thousands of dollars and pounds of equipment and move to a more fertile environment. As a renter, you can move freely from location to location and pick up the equipment you need where and when you need it.

It may sound as though buying equipment is too risky and restrictive for anyone who considers going into the business as his own boss. That is true only for some people, such as freelancers and independent producers. A business that might go into producing in-house training tapes, industrials, or merely documentation is best served by purchasing its own equipment. It makes perfect economic sense. If a business plans to shoot ten programs per year, rental might cost $25,000 for the whole works, including tape stock and personnel. That's not so far from the purchase price of a workable production package, and there still might be four good years of use in that new package. So buying is definitely the best deal for a company, no matter how large or small, that can guarantee a certain number of productions in the future.

For every new production company that succeeds, there are two that fail. And the reason has little to do with whether the companies in question rented or bought their equipment. You need a healthy list of clients who want your business, and it's a good idea to have one before you invest in a career in video as your own boss. You don't need a hundred hungry clients begging you to get into the business. As I said before, many video jobs result from contacts in the business and references from past jobs.

It's probable that you won't leap into ownership without first working in the field to scope it out. Once you've done that, and talked to people who might become potential clients, that is the time to make your move. A couple of regular clients who like working with you can guarantee a certain amount of work that can grease the wheels of your first year in business. Bosses who buy all the best equipment and then wait for the phone to ring are in for an unpleasant surprise. But if you do have a few clients and a good reputation, and you enhance that reputation with every job you take, it won't be long before you return your investment, whether it is time or money. Then you can make the step into purchasing your first equipment without worrying whether there is a market for it.

FINDING THAT FIRST JOB

It is highly unlikely that in your first job you will be your own boss. It takes time to get to know the market, the people, and video as a business. It is important to build your résumé and your contacts so that your career grows geometrically with the kind of work you do.

The first step in finding that first job is to play out every single contact that you ever made while you were in training. Of course, that assumes that you *made* some contacts while in training that you can use. In a school training situation, it's impossible not to make contacts of some kind. You'll be surrounded by fellow students who are learning the same things you are, and students are eager to share what they know and learn what others know. Probable contacts from school include students, teachers, and especially visiting professionals who come to lecture on campus. All of these people are fair game when it comes time to look for a job. Other students will be looking for jobs when you do, and some will find them. If somebody else found a job somewhere, maybe there's another one available for you.

Teachers usually are professionals who once worked in the video field. That means they have contacts in the business where they used to work. Your professor might be able to steer you to one or two places where he knows someone who needs a fresh face. If a teacher likes your work, he will probably suggest exactly that. Otherwise, it is up to you to get this information from your teacher.

Many colleges have a series of visiting professionals who come to classes and talk about their profession. As a rule, it is considered impolite to corner these poor souls and beg them for employment. Try to be tactful about it, asking thoughtful questions about employment possibilities in the business, or asking how she got her first job.

Cable stations that provide their own productions are prime candidates for that first job. If you've worked as an intern at a particular station, your chances are better. However, try to remember that the station will think twice before it pays you for something that it used to get free. It all depends on your performance. If the station *can't afford to lose you*, you've got a job. Otherwise they'll just fill your position with another free intern who can perform your duties.

If you haven't interned at a cable station, you can still get a job at one, providing you have some kind of credentials. Those credentials can be a degree in video production or something equivalent. Or you can start out in the office, get to know the place, familiarize yourself with the equipment in your free time, and then transfer into a department that is more to your liking. A cable station tends to have a high turnover because it is a training ground for so many people, and a high turnover means frequent openings. Try it.

The same principle that applies to finding a job at a cable station applies to finding one in larger companies with less turnover. The requirements of a local commercial TV station might be more stringent than those of the cable station, but the pay will be better and the opportunities greater, though they occur at a slower rate.

PUTTING TOGETHER YOUR RÉSUMÉ

The first thing you will need before you apply for a job anywhere is a résumé.

There are good résumés and there are bad résumés, and employers are suspicious of "great" résumés. If your credentials are so hot, why are you looking for work? There is no real trick to writing a good résumé; as long as it is concise, neatly organized, and legible, you've got as good a chance as anyone. A good résumé should have this information in this order

Name and address.

University and degree (if applicable).

Position desired.

Start with your most recent position and work down chronologically.

On the left side of the page, type the dates of your employment.

Next to the relevant date, state the position you held and underline it. Next to it, state where you held that job.

Using single space, write a *brief* description of your responsibilities. Nothing turns off a potential employer more than flowery prose describing how perfect you are.

Do the same all the way down the page and stop there.

Résumés should not exceed one page; most employers won't ever get to a second page when reading your résumé. Consider yourself lucky if they read it at all. Keep it short and simple. Here is a sample résumé:

Buster Baxter   University of Oneonta
555 Beanpole Ave.   B.A. in Broadcasting
Oneonta, North Dakota   Summa Cum Laude

Production Assistant

1992–97 Studio Manager, Wheeler Studios. Supervised three video studios during productions of commercials and television programs.

1991–92 Production Assistant, Wheeler Studios. Assisted the Floor Manager with multiple video productions.

1990–91 Intern Producer, Raven Cablevision. Introduced community programming to Oneonta and trained local organizations to use equipment and produce programming. Produced the long-running *Walks of Life* series.

1989–90 Production Assistant, KONE-TV Oneonta. Assisted film crew with production of public service spots.

1988–89 Video Specialist, Dept. of Broadcasting, Oneonta U. Supervised video equipment distribution and maintenance.

Do not feel compelled to fill up a page with meaningless details about jobs that don't relate to the job you are seeking. That means avoid any reference to that job as a bagger in your local supermarket. Stick to the relevant information. Also, it is obvious that Buster could have put "Studio Manager" or "Producer" as his heading, instead of "Production Assistant." But in this case, Buster was going for a job as a production assistant. He might use the same résumé and change the heading for a different job. If you know the position that you are going for, put it on top of your résumé, and the potential employer will assume you can do the job.

There are some tricks to résumé writing, none of which is guaranteed. It's a good practice to use a lot of verbs like "supervised," "organized," "completed," "researched" when describing your experience in the field. It gives the impression of action, as opposed to passive description.

A lot of job-seekers sweat over what color paper to choose for their résumé. It is true that black on white is not the greatest, and an off-white paper is a little classier. But avoid outlandish color schemes that distract the reader. White letters on green paper are about as effective as wearing a funny hat to your interview.

Sending Out Your Résumé

Type your résumé up nicely and make clean copies. Once you have a hefty stack of résumés, you have to decide where to send them. This is the time to let your fingers do the walking. Some of the larger video markets have paper-bound booklets that list products and services of every video business in town. The *MPE Motion Picture, TV, and Theater Directory* is published twice a year and lists, among the specific services, film and tape producers in all fifty states. You can order one by writing to Motion Picture Enterprises, Inc., Tarrytown, New York, 10591. The book isn't free, so call them at

212-245-0969 and ask how much. It's usually about five dollars, and worth ten times that amount. The booklet lists the producers and their addresses and phone numbers, which is all that you need to get started. Lacking that booklet, which isn't totally comprehensive, peruse the Yellow Pages directory under "Motion Picture Producers & Studios" and you'll find the same information.

Don't send your résumé to any of these places without a preliminary phone call. First call the place and ask if they are accepting résumés. You will usually get no further than the receptionist, who will say they aren't hiring but send it in anyway "for the files." This is like sending your résumé to a black hole in space, but it's still worth a try. The real reason that you call is to get the name and *correct spelling* of the person in charge of hiring. Make a list of the places to which you want to send your résumé and the appropriate names that go with them; then compose a separate cover letter for each one. Photocopied cover letters go right in the wastebasket with your résumé. Take the time to type a separate letter to an individual at each company. This provides a personal touch, and the employer feels obliged to read a personal letter.

A cover letter is simply a formal letter that states your intentions and interests. Here is one example:

Date

Barbara Howitzer, President
Blue Moon Productions

Dear Ms. Howitzer,

I am enclosing my résumé in the hope that you might be needing my services in the near future. I have a great deal of experience in video production, and I would like to bring that experience to Blue Moon Productions. I have heard that you need a good floor manager.

I will be in town for two days next week, and I would like to set up an appointment at your convenience. I will call you next Wednesday, and I look forward to meeting you.

>Sincerely,
>Buster Baxter

That might work and it might not. You never know. It helps to imply that you'll only be available for one or two days, which makes it impossible for the potential interviewer to put off appointments indefinitely.

Not only will your phone call be imminent, it should be relentless as well. People like Ms. Howitzer are very busy running a studio, and they don't often sit around waiting for us to call them and chat about future employment. You'll have to call and call. The worst that can happen is that she'll tell you there are no openings and to try in a couple of months "when things pick up." So call back in a couple of months and remind her of your conversation. This sort of persistence will get you more jobs than any résumé. She is likely to remember your persistence more than your dressed-up résumé. It is the traits that you show during job-seeking that tip off the employer as to what traits you'll bring to the job

When You Get an Interview

If you use the same determination for the fifteen or twenty potential employers, one of them will eventually invite you for an interview. This is when you have to shine! Dress up and look sharp. Greet your interviewer with a firm handshake and tell the truth.

Trust yourself. Tell them what you can do. If you have a demo reel, a compilation of your work (short and sweet!), *show* them what you can do. The rest is out of your hands—that is, after they make their decision. If you are put on hold, to be called later, a few more phone calls won't hurt. But once you have the interview, don't make yourself a pain by calling every hour to get the verdict. Be cool, but let them know that you have several other juicy offers that can't wait much longer.

You will go through several interviews like this before you get that first job. It might take months, maybe a year. Try to be patient. If someone offers you a job, make sure it is what you want to do; don't just leap at it blindly. If you take a job, you are committed to it, and walking out after three weeks because the job didn't meet your expectations can make your next job search even more difficult. When you get the job you want, congratulations! The wheels will turn and your career in video will be rolling.

PAYING DUES

There may be times when you are not able to pick and choose your job, especially the first one. It depends on your background. If your résumé is a bit sparse, it may be wise to take whatever is offered you. Many video professionals have past jobs on their résumé that they took only to put them there. Some jobs aren't all that much fun or exciting, or don't pay well, but might look swell when added to your résumé. In that case, take it if you need it. Consider it a pit stop along the way. Investing in a short-term job like that may pay off when going for the big job.

If your résumé *really* needs a boost, remember that someone is always willing to let you work for nothing. The lack of pay may make for some lean times that constitute "dues." A producer with his back against the wall on a production needs all the help he can get, and if you arrive at the right time you could be working right away. If you impress the producer, he'll remember you the next time around and remember your sacrifice. Maybe next time he'll get more money and hire you because if you worked so hard for nothing, think what you could do if you were paid!

The producer isn't the only one who might remember you and find work for you next time around. Every job you take is worth one more job for *each member* of the crew that you work with. Virtually everyone who goes on to the next job will be asked if he knows anybody who might be helpful, and your name could come up in the word-of-mouth lottery. That is why productive cooperation is so important in video production.

8

Rock and Reel

I hope my first film professor is reading this. We were wide-eyed college sophomores, hanging on your every word as you handed out the first film assignment. We had been successfully conditioned by obscure experimental films, watching an atomic explosion take place in slow motion at least fifty times in a row for two solid, silent hours. We got the picture: Film is Art, Art, Art. We set out in search of cinematic art, with your advice still ringing in our ears. "Whatever you do," you said, "don't make a film of your favorite song."

You should have said, "Choose a song. Go out and shoot yourself crazy. Use every technique in the book. Rifle the drawers of cinematic and television history. You won't even have to think about making a soundtrack. Cut wildly. Break the rules. In six years, movies with songs as the soundtrack will be the hottest thing to hit television."

The issue, of course, is music videos. Their venue started out to be late-night television programs. The videos were promotional tools, provided free of charge to the broadcaster, courtesy of the record company. Since the record company owned both the song and the performer, the only real expense was the production costs, which were anywhere from ten to fifty thousand dollars. If three hundred thousand people tuned in a popular television show and saw the promotional video, and just three percent of those viewers bought a record because of it, then the record company recouped its investment plus profit. And the total sales numbers topped that three percent by a long shot.

So it is no great gamble for the record companies to give away their videos to television production companies. The television producers know a good thing when they see one, and free broadcast material featuring sassy superstars mouthing their latest hit is certainly a good thing. Why, you could broadcast that kind of stuff all day and all night, like a radio station, while the record companies foot the bill for the bulk of the production budget. That is exactly what MTV has done.

The euphoric fascination with music videos has since peaked and leveled off. The result is that the record companies have trimmed the budget allowed each music video. You could say "Shucks" to that, shake your head, and go looking for the next trend. But the fact is that the leveling off, the lower budgets, and the inevitable standardization of music videos work in favor of those who would like to work in the field.

Some of the more shortsighted and euphoric producer/directors of music videos became so giddy about what they perceived as a bottomless pot of gold that they priced their services very, very high, hoping to haul in some of that business. When the record companies lowered the boom, many high rollers found the rolling a little lonely. Still, more videos are made today than ever before, and the percentage of good ones has increased dramatically. Somebody is getting an awful lot of work, and it might as well be you.

It is a rare performer or musical group that refuses to make a video to promote a record. For the unknown group, a video is a necessity. It is cheaper and faster than touring, and a video can literally make an unknown group into a hot commodity in a matter of weeks.

The music video is primarily the director's domain. Record companies are looking for nothing but fresh ideas married to an exciting sound. You, as a director, cannot affect the sound of a particular group, but a clever idea can give the group instant recognition and credibility.

No matter where you are, what size city or town, there is at least one band pounding away in a basement or garage. Bars and clubs have to turn away as many groups as they employ. If the group is doing original music, all you have to do is give a listen, assess the value of the song and the appeal of the group, and come up with a good idea for a video.

Approach the band with your idea. If they like it, you'll have to find the money to make the video. This is where the good idea will save money that more established bands spend on production pizzazz.

You could shoot the video on anything from consumer-quality half-inch VHS or Beta to Super-8 film. The "home movie look" is currently in vogue, most probably as a backlash to the slick productions that have lost their appeal. You can use this trend to your advantage. If you shoot your video on the cheap, as they say, you can be hip and efficient at the same time.

The music video's great advantage is that the soundtrack is already complete. The song provides the music, the message, and the beat with which to time your cuts.

You will save money by avoiding lip-synching to the song. Many good videos are made without lip synch, and some are more interesting because of it. But if you must have it, here is how it's done.

You need what is called "playback." The idea behind playback is that the playback machine plays a tape of the song *at exactly the same speed every time the song is played.* This is imperative because, as you may not know, home tape recorders play at a slightly different speed each time, and no two consumer tape decks play at exactly the same speed. The variance is subtle, inaudible to the ear, but it makes an enormous difference when the singer's lips don't quite match up.

The ideal playback machine is the Nagra tape recorder. Built into the Nagra is a *servo-controlled motor.* The servo insures that the tape speed never varies, even as the batteries weaken. Sony makes a cassette recorder with a servo motor, and it works equally well at less cost.

Plug the tape player into your video or film recorder. Play the song. Sing along. You're halfway home to a music video.

Once you have your footage, take the same tape player and the same tape to an editing facility. Plug the tape player into the editing system, and record the song onto your master editing tape. Now you have a tape with a soundtrack that runs at the same speed as the soundtrack on your visuals.

At this point, all you have to do is lay pictures over the soundtrack. When you need the lip synch portion, you'll have to match the music recorded on the visuals to the music recorded on the master tape. If you don't have or can't afford the sophisticated machinery to make this work, don't despair. Simply choose a beat in the music and find it on both tapes. You will be in relative synch. All it takes is a little fine tuning and a good ear.

I recommend shooting the entire song with your talent lip-synching all the way through. Then lay that footage over the soundtrack on your edit tape. This way, your lip-synch work is done. Now you can simply insert nonsynch visuals where you don't want to see the singer.

This is an overly basic and rudimentary approach to making a music video, but it represents the foundations of the format. It is a good and simple exercise for any aspiring filmmaker, especially since music videos permit great freedom for experimentation.

Treat your finished music video as you would a résumé. Send it to producers, record companies, contests, festivals, the works. Follow up with phone calls and interviews when possible.

Most music videos that you see are made by established production companies that specialize in the field. They became established by making a few videos and developing a style. When a record company decides which style best suits a particular group, they contract the appropriate production company to produce the video. Therefore, the production companies are your main targets for finding employment.

Alas, those companies are located where the record companies are located, and that means New York and Los Angeles, with emphasis on the latter. Even the smallest record company, which might be more inclined to hire the novice independent producer to make a low-budget music video, will be camped out in one of the big cities.

The employment outlook for production specialists, such as camera operators, production managers, gaffers, stylists, and so on is excellent when it comes to music video production. Scores of freelancers water their dry spells with the occasional music video, because the production schedule is short and intense, and the final product is highly visible.

The majority of music videos are edited on tape at various production houses across the country. Post-production houses are happy to have them because of the high volume of productions, and because most music videos need at least a minimum of expensive special effects.

The world of animation has found new life, thanks to music videos. There is a tremendous need for talented graphic artists who are willing to learn and become proficient at the animation technology currently in use. It is like painting with a computer keyboard instead of a brush or pen. Music videos have allowed animators to work freely with the new technology, and the result is the advent of high-tech animation that is just beginning to bloom. As animated music videos proliferate, more performers want one of their own. Animation promises much more control and a highly stylized look.

Those are the two most important aspects of music video production: low budget and high visibility. Both work to the advantage of everybody. New, fresh ideas are in constant demand, due to the voracious appetite of networks such as MTV. Rock, country, and even jazz are all dependent on the music video for world-wide promotion. And a little experience goes a long way.

Music videos are not a fad that will wither and die. Record companies are committed to the music video for one simple reason: money. The reason that a rock group goes on tour is to promote their latest record. Tours are monstrous things, requiring intensive organization and lots of money. A music video achieves the same thing at a fraction of the cost. There are too many records and too many bands for one person or company to make all the videos, and new acts are coming up all the time. There stands to be a lot of work in the field for a long time.

For the majority of directors, the music video is a good way to keep working, keep visible, and develop a snazzy demo reel. The format has been tested by everyone from backyard amateurs to well-known film directors like Brian De Palma and Sam Peckinpah. The videos are not taken very seriously, so you can have a lot of fun and freedom while making one.

If you can't find a band to work with you, go through your record and tape collection. Choose one of your favorite songs. Make a movie of it.

For an extensive listing of companies involved in various aspects of music video, consult *The Rockamerica Guide to Video/Music*. It can be purchased from Rockamerica, Inc., 119 West 22nd Street, New York, NY 10011.

It is only fair to warn those aspiring music video directors/producers/etceteras: As we hip-hop into the twenty-first century, the music video business appears to have aged horribly overnight. Although the consumer is certainly unaware of it, hostility is growing within the television production industry, and those ill feelings are directed towards the *dedicated* music video producer.

If you are a video cameraman, and you walk into a job interview and declare that you're worked on Rockvideo X and Rockvideo Y and Rockvideo Z, your potential employer is going to say to you or himself, "What else is new?" Most professionals are all too aware of the fact that music video cinematography is tremendously forgiving; there is no stylistic consistency, and the quick cutting provides a handy Bandaid for any shooting mistakes. Potential employers have taken to asking for a cameraman's *rushes*, which is the unedited footage, where every mistake and glitch is painfully evident. Be prepared for that. Always approach every job, no matter how small, with maximum concentration and professionalism.

Get some variety on your reel. You have to get those industrials and commercials and documentaries and corporate spots on your reel to prove that you can work with all types of clients, and not just your friends or your age group. Mix it up a little, and you'll triple your work. Go ahead and experiment on those music videos; that's what they are good for. But it's no good reason to be faithful to them.

9

The Tough Get Started

Broadcasting a news event is like playing the game of "telephone": As the news of an event spreads, it resembles the original event less and less. But a larger audience is able to participate in the event. As that audience increases, the individual members of the audiences have less in common.

In order to make up for this gap, television dresses itself in the latest and most expensive fashions. The use of outlandish special effects has turned every image into a metallic construction. The hi-tech advancement of video effects has suddenly shifted into high gear because of the improvements in digital video. Computerized graphics keep an image interesting until they develop a newer, more expensive way to render the same image.

The end result of all this celebrated advancement in television technology is that the newest equipment is now so expensive that most universities cannot afford them, yet these systems are standard equipment at most mid-sized television production studios. Every technological advancement in video that increases the cost of the system also increases the distance between the video student and professional experience.

Do not despair, faithful reader. We can get right around that nonsense. If the television industry decides to make its favorite toys unavailable to you, let them go right ahead. What they are doing is leading themselves away from the purpose of television. While they are doing that, they are leaving a nice big space for you to fill.

What you need to do is become proficient in the basics of true television. Then, as you move ahead in your career, your peers will hand you the tools and the technology to achieve that end. Your goal will be to communicate with your community. I'll use the high school or undergraduate university as our model community.

There are things happening in your community. That is *news*. Maybe something really big just happened, which is more important or compelling than the other things. That is the *lead story*. If a dance is coming up, or a big ball game, or a play, that is your *soft news*, or your entertainment. Maybe your science teacher just grew the world's first cross-eyed tomato. Make him your *human interest* story. If the principal is having an affair with Mr. Goodwrench, make that your exposé, or your *feature story*. We're here to have fun, remember?

What you are about to build is a television program with a *magazine format*. The magazine format television show uses virtually every potential approach and execution of nonfiction television production: research, writing, planning, shooting, lighting, performing, editing, ad sales, and distribution. The structure is simple, the style is accessible and familiar, the sources of material are infinite, and the material is suited for a small audience.

THE TELEVISION MAGAZINE FORMAT
1. Opening sequence
2. The "table of contents"
3. The lead story
4. News stories

THE TOUGH GET STARTED

5. Feature story
6. The roundup
7. Previews of next show
8. Closing

This format will require preproduction (research, writing, reporting, organizing, and artwork); production (lighting, shooting, audio, and performance); and postproduction (editing, music and voice mix, and presentation).

The place to start is in sales. You have to sell your program to whomever will provide the facilities. If your high school or college has a modest television production facility or the basic equipment, your job is easier. If not, sell your idea to your local TV station, which might be public access cable, an independent station, or a network affiliate. Do not presume that they will broadcast your program. You just want to use their equipment to reach your small audience.

Give your program a name. Then sell the purpose: to inform and entertain the student body while generating important video experience for the participants. Each and every role in the production should be filled by a different student each week, so that every student has a chance to learn every aspect, regardless of sex, race, experience, or ego.

Divide your group into four teams: advertising, writing and research, production, and postproduction.

Advertising Team

Advertising is your secret weapon. You may have difficulty selling your program if your provider hasn't the funds to back your production. You can use your community audience to your advantage. Since the community is small, it's easier for your advertising team to research that audience and discover what they like to eat, wear, watch, and do with what little "disposable income" they have. If they like Fred's Hamburgers, go to Fred and tell him that you've got his audience in your pocket and he should maintain his strong position as a leading hamburger provider for that audience.

Once you have a select group of advertisers, it's up to the advertising team to develop a campaign for each advertiser. Keep it modest and simple. I recommend art cards for each one. Have your artists draw or paint a handful of creative cards, or maybe the advertiser will provide a photo. The advertiser may select one of those, or you may use them all and rotate them from show to show. Develop some basic copy, or narration, for each one, consulting with the advertiser for ideas and crucial information such as prices and location. Deliver the artwork and the basic copy to the writing team.

The Writing Team

The writers will have their hands full. You may want to subdivide this group into three units: advertising copy, news copy, and host copy.

The advertising unit takes what has been provided by the advertising team and works with them to develop creative copy for each commercial. Work within a thirty- or sixty-second time frame and use a stopwatch to time your efforts. Don't be shy about using sound effects and music, or more than one voice per spot. Listen to radio commercials for ideas, since your visuals will not carry the ball as well as the visuals in a slick high-budget commercial.

The news team will carry the burden of the work. The first step is to find the stories, and that will take an alert eye and the nose of a bloodhound. Set a limit on the number of stories to cover, which might be six, including the lead story. Assign a writer to each story. The

The Tough Get Started

writer gathers all the information about his story, does interviews, and writes it as a news story. You then have two options for each story: you can assign a location crew to shoot supporting video footage for the story, or you can assign the art department to make up a graphic that illustrates the story.

You might have two hosts who will anchor the program. The hosts for that show should be part of the writing team and responsible for their own copy. Assign the lead story to one host and the feature story to the other. Do not neglect the little things that make a show run smoothly, such as the introduction to the show and the small farewells and welcomes that get you in and out of commercials.

Once the writers have developed the stories for the given program, the package is delivered to the production team.

The Production Team

It is up to the production team's director to decide what order to impose on the material. Start with the most important and save the most interesting for last. Then the director makes the decision whether to support the story with video or a graphic, and that depends on the availability of location equipment and the demands of the schedule. Once those decisions have been made, it's time to fire up the lights and roll tape.

Build the show in units that will be ultimately assembled by the editors. I cannot recommend attempting a live broadcast because the chances are that neither your studio nor your personnel is equipped for such an undertaking. You will be able to focus your efforts on each unit and produce it to your best abilities without the added pressure of live performance.

Shoot everything that the hosts must do at once. That means the introduction, their stories, the commercial breaks, and the closing. That way, you'll only have to light them and record them once. What makes it difficult for the hosts is that they must pretend that the show is live, and the demands of that type of performance might require more than one attempt. Keep a record of each take, and mark the one that you intend to use. Send the tape and your notes to the editors.

Shoot all the advertising art cards and news graphics at the same time as well. This is a good chance for the cameraman to practice zooms and pans on a static object. Again, this tape should be delivered to the editors with a precise list of each chart and the order in which they were recorded.

If possible, while you are shooting in the studio your location crews are outside shooting the supporting video and interviews. Each crew should have the attendant writer/reporter on hand to outline the story for the cameraman so that his images are in line with the story. It is up to the reporter to keep a record of the footage and deliver the tape with notes to the editors.

In the studio the audio crew records the reporter's voice-overs, the commercial voice-overs, and any music or sound effects, all on a videotape.

At the end of the production schedule, the editors should have received the following tapes: the host/anchors, graphics, location footage, and audio. I cannot stress strongly enough the importance of clear and accurate notes, called *log sheets*, that must accompany every videotape. It is a criminal act just to dump videotape on an editor without telling him or her where anything is and expect the editor to fish through hours of footage trying to figure out what you were up to. If you want your story to come out the way you intended, see to it that your instructions are clear.

The Postproduction Team

The editor has the tapes, the log sheet for each take, and a program outline that assigns an order to the program. The first order of business is to edit each individual story down to a finished unit. That means marrying the picture with voice and/or music.

Once all the units have been completed, get out the stop-watch and time every one. Add up those times and pray that the show adds up to the desired program length, which should be thirty minutes. Few broadcast programs are longer than thirty minutes, and you should learn to work within professional parameters. Depending upon the number and length of your commercials, you should wind up with nearly twenty-three minutes of actual program time. Time it down to the last second.

The chances are good that the editor will have to go back and trim or lengthen a segment of the show to make it fit the desired length. This is where true creative resourcefulness comes in. Don't allow writers anywhere near you as you are fine-tuning the segments. They will defend their segments against all others and make you miserable. Lock the door and assemble all the units into one program.

The presentation of the show may be over the local television channel, or a closed-circuit dorm channel, or simply a television set up in the student lounge. Wherever it is, you can bet that your community's interest in your work will be high. Broadcast television has proven time and again how the placement of a video camera in front of virtually anything can make it seem more important, and you will find that to be true of the subjects of your program. Once you have established yourself as a regular program, stories will come to you. That will make your job both easier and harder: less legwork to find the stories, more brainwork to make intelligent choices.

The glory of your efforts will be short-lived. As everybody in the newspaper business knows, yesterday's ground-breaking article is today's handy dandy training tool for housebreaking a puppy. No sooner will your host say "Goodnight" than the gears will start turning and the schedule start humming and the pressure build on the demands of the next program.

That kind of pressure, along with the steady hunger of television, is what a career in professional video is all about. You'll soon be accustomed to the pressure and be prepared for your chosen career. In the meantime, you'll find that the production of a magazine format television program will keep you on top and in tune with everything that happens in your community. As your expertise increases, so will your professional and social contacts, and never again will you be able to look at broadcast television the same way. You will inevitably notice that the networks are doing exactly what you are doing, only they have more expensive tools with which to produce their shows.

Don't be intimidated by the glitz of network television. Just as the basic video camera is your current tool, so will the latest incarnation of the ADO be your tool in the future. By learning and practicing what counts, by *communicating with your audience*, you will inevitably further your career in video, and you will recognize the high-tech tools as conveniences.

By the time you have completed production of a few programs, you are likely to discover yourself gravitating toward one particular area of video production. Before you focus completely on that area, keep your eyes open to all the other areas so you can see how they affect your chosen area of expertise. It is equally likely that somebody else, such as your teacher or counselor or a fellow student, will notice that you excel in one area when you weren't even aware of it. Heed those compliments and follow your instincts. Instinct is the one thing that they cannot program into even the most expensive special-effects generator.

10

The Digital Video Revolution

There is nothing but good news in the new developments in video production. Digital video is, to put it simply, another way to organize a video picture so that it can be easily manipulated. The electronic signal, instead of becoming imprinted on the oxide of a tape magnetically, can now be encoded as 1's and 0's—the currency of the digital world. This method is called digital compression.

What does this mean to you, as a producer, director, editor, cameraman, or graphic artist? What it means is that now there are more avenues that your production—or career—can take. New arenas are now opening up in multimedia, interactive television programming, CD-ROM development, and the internet, to name just a few hot zones. The appetite for video products is huge and getting larger. And there is one very simple secret that should bring a smile to the face of anyone embarking on a career in video.

Open any book on the subject of digital video production, and it will tell you that the images that are needed for these new arenas are produced in exactly the same way that they have been described to you in this book. You will still plan and shoot your video. You may still shoot on tape, or maybe onto a digital disk; no matter, the same rules apply.

Digital compression squeezes your video so that it fits on a computer's hard drive, or a CD-ROM, or a Digital Video Disk. The technology that allows that compression to happen is changing by the minute, but unless you intend to pursue a career in computer engineering, you need not concern yourself too much with the minute aspects of digital technology. You may, as a producer, need to tweak your video, while shooting, so that the material isn't too complex for the current compression scheme. In general, though, you will simply forge ahead with your video production, thanking your lucky stars that now you have so many new ways to distribute your work.

Editors, as I've mentioned earlier, need to learn a different system of editing, working in the new, superior non-linear way. But the fundamentals remain the same; intelligent and creative assembly of pictures that best realizes the vision of the director.

The greatest opportunity in accessible digital technology is for the graphic artist. The emergence of graphic elements such as type, animation, and even special effects has changed the look of everything from broadcast television to the latest cool site on the Web. Producers are using these elements to great advantage, and the demand for creative artists who can manipulate graphic imagery and type has skyrocketed.

But perhaps the greatest news on this front is that digital technology is now cheaper than ever, and therefore you can now learn and practice the basics of computer graphics, and even video editing, on your home or school computer. Special effects packages, for example, which used to require a bank loan and a trust fund in order to buy three hours at the local production facility, are now available to you as off-the-shelf software. These programs work *exactly the same* as the big rigs at the facilities, and, in fact, the availability of these programs, such as Adobe After Effects and Photoshop, is putting some of the older facilities out of business.

The tools for video production have become cheaper than ever before, and more accessible to you. Remember that the basics of video production—planning, writing, shooting, editing—are the same as they have been since the old Hollywood days of D.W. Griffith and Charlie Chaplin. What has been changed most dramatically by the digital revolution is the editing process, the style, and especially the market for your finished production, and your talents. Every technical advance just pushes the door open a little wider for you. Step in and see what you can do.

Appendix

MAGAZINES

A few magazines are available that can give you a good insight into what's happening in the world of video. These are professional magazines that nearly every production facility will have strewn around their offices. Go to one of these places and ask for some old issues. Or go to a comprehensive magazine store and pick up a few. Give 'em a look and if you like what you see, order a subscription. It's worth keeping up to date.

American Cinematographer
International Journal of Film and Video Production Techniques
1782 North Orange Drive
Hollywood, CA 90028

Monthly
Feature film-oriented, but a good place to read about tricks of the trade, chock full of profiles and specialties such as special effects. Best for the aspiring cameraperson.

Backstage
The Complete Service Weekly for the Communications and Entertainment Industry

Backstage Publications
330 West 42nd Street
New York, NY 10036

Backstage West
5150 Wilshire Boulevard
Los Angeles, CA 90036

Backstage Midwest
841 North Addison Avenue
Elmhurst, IL 60126

Weekly
A newspaper with a slant toward the business end of production, *Backstage* consists mostly of news about facilities all over the country and their latest accomplishments. Seldom presents anything controversial, and almost always puffs even the most inconsequential production. But there are listings for job opportunities, and the weekly format can keep you up to date on who is expanding and might need employees. Regular departments include equipment news, business screen, animation, music notes, agency news and views, West, Midwest, and Florida markets, and theater and casting. Worth a look at 75¢.

DV (Digital Video Magazine)
411 Borel Ave., Suite 100
San Mateo, California 94402
(415) 358-9500
http://www.dv.com
$4.95
Slick, smart, less promotional and more professional than most consumer mags. For real wire-heads.

On Location
The Film and Videotape Production Magazine
6777 Hollywood Boulevard
Suite 501
Hollywood, CA 90028

Monthly
Expensive ($3.50), slick and glossy, and covers all of the angles with a wide range of regular departments that include commercials, video, audio, production news, music video, and equipment updates. Articles are written by professionals.

Variety
"The Bible of the Entertainment Industry"

Weekly
A mind-boggling collection of news and features and plentiful advertisements. You must read this, if only to find out who is running the show out there. Available everywhere.

Videomaker
P.O. Box 4591
Chico, CA, 95927
(916) 891-8410
FAX (916) 891-8443
http://www.videomaker.com
$2.95
Videomaker's mission is to democratize and enrich television by educating, inspiring, and informing end users. This is one excellent magazine. Good mix of utility features and reviews. Go to school on it.

VideoPro
P.O. Box 5044
Westport, CT 06881

Monthly
Good buy at $2.00, strictly video with features by pros about all aspects of video, especially new developments. Regular departments include newsbreaks, facilities

around the U.S. and what is happening at each one, personnel news, and good product/equipment updates.

Millimeter
Subscription Dept.
826 Broadway
New York, NY 10003

Monthly
Feature film-oriented, $3.25, focuses on the really big film productions, but worthwhile for its detailed articles written by directors, cameramen, etc., about a particular production and how it was achieved. Departments include production industry news, teleproduction news, motion picture news, and projects that are "in production." Oriented to the advertising agency.

Books
If you want to study video in more depth, particularly the technology, here are a few books that can give you a basic overview.

Grob, Bernard. *Basic Television.* New York: McGraw-Hill, Inc. 1964.
Still effective as a technical handbook.

Lipton, Lenny. *Independent Filmmaking,* rev. ed. San Francisco: Straight Arrow Books, 1973.
Written for independent filmmakers, but videomakers can get some insight from his elementary description of the technology, as well as his freewheeling philosophy of independent production.

Shure, A. *Basic Television,* Vol. 1. New York: John F. Rider, 1958.
Even more basic than Bernard Grob's version, and easier to read.

White, Gordon. *Video Recording*. London: Newnes Butter-worths, 1971.
An overview of all kinds of recording systems, written by an engineer.

Marsh, Ken. *Independent*. San Francisco: Straight Arrow Books, 1974.
Billed as "A complete guide to the physics, operation, and application of the new television for the student, the artist, and for community TV," *Independent* reads like a Whole Video Catalog, complete with inexact drawings. But a good bet for a basic understanding.

Educational Programs

Here is a list of some of the Intern/Training/Apprentice Programs available in the U.S. It is by no means comprehensive. For more information, try the latest edition of *Gadney's Guide to International Contests, Festivals and Grants*, Festival Publications, P.O. Box 10180, Glendale, CA 91209

AAAS Mass Media Intern Program
American Association for the Advancement of Science
1776 Massachusetts Avenue, NW
Washington, DC 20036
Open to social/natural science college students.

Alternate Media Center Apprenticeship Grant Program
New York University School of the Arts
144 Bleecker Street
New York, NY 10012
Open to all, with local sponsors.

CPB Training Grants
Corporation for Public Broadcasting
1111 16th Street, NW

Washington, DC 20036
Open to U.S. women and minorities through public broadcast TV/radio stations.

Grass-Roots Intern Program
Grass Roots Network
Box 2006
Aspen, CO 81611
Open to all.

PBS/Ford Scholar Management Internships
Ford Foundation
Office of Communications
320 East 43rd Street
New York, NY 10017
Open to public TV employees.

Film/Video Arts Training, Internship, and Equipment Loan Programs
817 Broadway
New York, NY 10003

JOURNALISM/NEWS
Alfred I. Dupont–Columbia University Awards in Broadcast Journalism
Columbia University
Graduate School of Journalism
New York, NY 10027

SCHOOLS
Nearly every university or college offers a program or degree in television, but not all of them are great. Contact the school that you are interested in and inquire about the available degree and the status of the available equipment.

A few schools offer really outstanding Film/TV/Broadcasting programs. They are:

APPENDIX

U.C.L.A., Los Angeles, California

New York University, New York

Columbia University, New York

University of Southern California

University of Iowa, Iowa City, Iowa

Southern Illinois University, Edwardsville, Illinois

University of Texas at Austin

University of Missouri/Columbia (Journalism only), Columbia, Missouri

Index

A
advertising agency, 38
advertising sales, 122, 123–124
aggressiveness, 89–90
Allen, Woody, 71
angle, camera, 69, 70
animation, 118
art cards, 124, 126
art director, 39–40, 43
artwork, 124
assistant director (AD), 31–32, 35, 50
assistant producer, 27–28, 41
attitude, toward job, 26, 88, 89
audio engineer, 56–61, 73–74, 82, 94

B
backing, financial, 27, 35
barndoor, 63, 64
Begin, Menachem, 22
boom operator, 55
boss, being your own, 100–112
budget, production, 4, 9, 27, 34, 35, 114

C
cable
 access studio, 16–19, 23, 24
 air time, 17
 specialization, 6
 station, 105
camera, 5, 28, 31, 54–55, 62
 hand-held, 74
 TV, 21, 54, 126
camera operator, 21, 51, 55, 60, 66, 67, 68–76, 94, 117, 119
 and editor, 78
 and ENG, 76
 and gaffer, 67–68
 staff, vs. free-lance, 96–97
cassette, 1, 59
CBS, 22–23
CD-ROM, 130, 131
Chaplin, Charlie, 69, 132
character generator (CG) operator, 83–84
client
 demands of, 30, 37, 91
 and editor, 82
 free-lance, 97
 list, 103
close-up, 69, 78
clothespins, 64
college, training at, 12–16, 23, 24
color, in lighting, 62–63
commercial, TV, 11, 27, 28, 29, 38, 125
 and character generator, 83
 director, 29
 photographer, 75
 writer, 38
communication, 15, 28, 122, 128
computer, 77, 79–80, 82, 86, 132–133
 graphics, 131
 painting on, 118
consistency, 90
contacts
 making, 15, 104–105
 using, 27, 33, 47, 103, 104
control booth, 51
copywriter, 38
corporate spot, 119
costs
 education, 15–16
 equipment, 101–102, 103–104, 121

INDEX

film production, 4, 11
video, 4, 12, 27, 115
cover letter, 109–110
creativity, 30, 38, 82
crew
  ENG, 60, 73–74, 75–76
  preproduction, 27, 41
  production, 9, 30, 31, 35, 44, 45, 46
Cronkite, Walter, 22
curriculum, media, 12–13

D

demo reel, 111, 118
De Palma, Brian, 119
dependability, of video, 4
determination, 89, 92, 110
diffusion filter, 63
digital
  compression, 79–80, 130, 131
  disk, 130
  technology, 131
  video, 2, 130
  video production, 130
director, 3, 9, 21, 25, 28–31, 32, 37, 39, 50, 51, 53, 70–71
  and camera operator, 70–71, 75
  and editor, 81
  music video, 114, 115
documentary, 27, 29, 34–35, 119
  lighting, 62
  photography, 75–76
  script, 38
downtime, computer, 78

E

Edison, Thomas, 8
editing
  non-linear, 79–80, 131
  off-line system, 79
  on-line system, 81
  postproduction, 11, 13, 37, 81, 122, 123, 126–127
editor, 32, 34, 78–81, 85
  internship, 24
electricity, knowledge of, 64–65

Electronic News Gathering (ENG), 60, 73–74, 75–76
engineer, 76–78, 81, 102
equipment, 35
  buying vs. renting, 101–104
  and engineer, 76–78
  learning, 14, 17
  maintenance, 101–102
  obsolete, 16, 18, 101
experience
  gaining, 13, 15, 17
  industry, 16
  professional, 19–20
exposure, film, 3
  automatic, 5, 66

F

feature story, 122, 125
film, 3, 4, 5, 65
fishing reel, 55
flag, 63
floor manager, 50–51
focus, 69, 70
footage, 78, 116
free-lancer, 96–97, 98, 103, 117

G

gaffer, 61–68, 117
  and camera operator, 75
gel, 63
goals, consideration of, 25, 87
"gopher," 25, 45
graphic artist, 49–50, 124, 130, 131
graphic equalizer, 60
graphics
  computerized, 121
  news, 125, 126
Griffith, D. W., 132
group, musical, 114, 117

H

hand-held mic, 57
hands-on
  experience, 23

labor, 40
training, 13
Hitchcock, Alfred, 69
Hollywood, 8, 9
hosts, program, 32, 124, 125–126
human interest story, 122

I
imagination, 89
immediacy, of video, 4
improvisation, 88–89
industrial, 27, 29, 49, 75, 76, 103, 119
    script, 36, 37–38
interactive television programming, 130
internet, 130
internship, 19–24, 88
    disadvantages of, 21–22, 23–24
    local TV station, 19–21
interview, job, 110–111

J
job
    first, 12, 47, 104–112
    with local TV station, 19–21
    nonpaying, 21, 22
    -seeking, 89, 90
    staff, 96–97
    where to find, 8–11
journalism, college, 14

L
lavalier mic, 57–58
leadership, assuming, 15
lead story, 122, 125
lighting
    and camera, 65–67
    design, 13, 40
    of video production, 61–67, 122, 123
light meter, 66–67
lights, 34, 63
limiter, 5
line producer, 32–33, 34
lipsynching, 115–116

location
    alternate, 42
    choosing business, 100–101
    interior, 64–65
    scouting for, 13
    shooting on, 9, 11, 18, 40, 42, 43, 44, 48, 52, 57, 64, 72–73, 98
log sheets, 126, 127

M
magazine format, 75, 76, 122–125, 128
makeup artist, 40
media department, college, 12
Meyer, Nicholas, 9–10
microphone, 56–59, 60, 73
mind, analytical, 30
mistakes, learning from, 13–14
mixing board, 59, 60
monitor
    playback, 3
    preview, 51, 54
    TV, 51, 54, 66
motion picture, feature, 9, 11, 28, 40
    made-for-TV, 28
MPE Motion Picture, TV, and Theater Directory, 108
multimedia, 2, 130
music video, 113–120

N
narrative
    camera work, 75
    lighting, 62
    script, 36, 37, 38, 48
nepotism, 25
network
    affiliate, 11, 23
    series, 11
    TV, 7, 54
news program, TV, 22–23, 49–50, 54, 55, 57, 72, 73–74, 76, 122–129

INDEX

P
patience, 18, 90–91, 93, 94
Peckinpaugh, Sam, 119
perfectionist, 93
performing, 122, 123
permit, shooting, 42
playback deck, 79, 80, 115–116
postproduction, 13, 18, 24, 78–86, 100, 117, 123, 127
preproduction, 27, 31, 64, 67, 123
pressure, programming, 128
producer, 26–27, 36, 39, 45, 102, 103, 111–112
  college, 14
  local, 12
  low-budget, 5
  nonbroadcast, 3–4
  public-access, 17
production
  in college training, 13, 15
  company, 117–118
  ENG, 73
  film, 11, 55
  live, 52
  low-budget, 52, 73
  nonbroadcast, 3, 31
  nontechnical, 26–51
  organization for, 13
  technical, 51–78
  television, 11, 24, 32, 121, 122, 128
production assistant (PA), 45–47, 107–108
production manager (PM), 27, 40–45, 46, 94, 117
professional
  determined, 92
  video, 47
  visiting, 104–105
programming
  cable, 6
  local organization, 6, 12
  public access, 16–18
  radio, 6
  television, 6, 29
promotional, 4, 49, 75, 76, 113
property master, 48–49
proposal, grant, 27
  writing, 35–36
props, 40, 48–49
public service announcement, 27

R
radio, 6
  microphone, 58, 59–60
record company, 113–114, 115, 117, 118
record deck, 79, 80
reporter, 60, 126
  ENG, 73–75
  investigate, 33
researcher, 27, 33–35, 122, 123
resourcefulness, 88, 89
résumé, 106–109, 110, 111, 117
rewards, of video industry, 96–99
Rockamerica Guide to Video/Music, 119
rushes, 119

S
schedule
  shooting, 35, 39, 42
  synchronizing, 13
  time, 29
schools, film, 9, 15
screenplay, writing, 36
script, 27, 36, 81
  shooting, 31, 35, 39, 75
  supervisor, 39
  writer, 36
set
  decor, 40
  designer, 40, 48
  lighting, 61, 75
  wrapping, 50
shoot
  delegation of duties, 13
  elements of, 13
  organizing, 13, 14
shooting, 122, 123
  location, 11
  studio, 11

shotgun mic, 57, 60
soap opera, 55, 81
soft news, 122
sound level, 59, 60
soundman, 56, 73
  (See also *audio engineer*)
sound mixer, 82
soundtrack, 115, 116
source, sound, 59
special effects generator (SEG) operator, 84–85
special effects software packages, 131–132
strip-chart, 41–42
studio shooting, 44, 48, 50, 59
switcher, 51–52, 81

T
talent, 30, 31, 39, 57–59
  coordinator, 27, 32–33
talk show, 27, 32, 48, 57
tape
  master, 51, 79, 116
  obituary, 23
  reel-to-reel, 59
  training, 4, 103
tape recorder, video, 1, 3, 4, 53–55, 77, 79–80
TBC processing amplifier, 80
team, production, 17
  professional, 19
technical director (TD), 51–53
technology, video, 6, 12, 17
Ted Turner Enterprises, 6
television
  broadcast, 6
  cable, 6
  as "illustrated radio," 61
  station, local, 12, 19–24, 105, 123, 127
time
  competition for, 18
  satellite, 22–23
Time, Inc., 6
tools, knowing your, 89
training, acquiring, 12–25, 87–88
travel, opportunities for, 98
treatment, writing, 35
troubleshooting, 88, 89

U
union
  pay, 96–97
university, training at, 12–16, 87–88

V
video
  animator, 118
  deck, 76–77
  editing, 131
  footage, 125, 126
  production, 2, 130–131
  tap, 54–55
voice-over, 37–38, 126
VTR operator, 53–55, 94

W
[World Wide] Web, 131
Willis, Gordon, 67, 71
wireless mic, 58
writer, 27, 35–39
writing, 122, 123, 124, 125